Painting and Decorating

NVQ and Technical Certificate Level 2

carillion

www.heinemann.co.uk

✓ Free online support
✓ Useful weblinks
✓ 24 hour online ordering

01865 888058

Heinemann

Inspiring generations

Heinemann, Halley Court, Jordan Hill, Oxford OX2 8EJ

Heinemann is the registered trademark of Harcourt Ltd

© Carillion Construction Ltd

First published 2006

11 10 09 08 07 06
10 9 8 7 6 5 4 3 2 1

British Library Cataloguing in Publication Data is available
from the British Library on request.

10-digit ISBN: 0 435 46359 4
13-digit ISBN: 978 0 43546359 5

Designed by HL Studios
Layout by HL Studios
Printed in the UK by Scotprint
Illustrated by HL Studios

Cover design by GD Associates
Cover photo: © Harcourt Ltd/Gareth Boden and Jane Hance

Websites

Please note that the examples of websites suggested in this book were up-to-date at the time of writing. We have made all links available on the Heinemann website at www.heinemann.co.uk/hotlinks. When you access the site, the express code is 3594P.

The information and activities in this book have been prepared according to the standards reasonably to be expected of a competent trainer in the relevant subject matter. However, you should be aware that errors and omissions can be made and that different employers may adopt different standards and practices over time. Therefore, before doing any practical activity, you should always carry out your own Risk Assessment and make your own enquiries and investigations into appropriate standards and practices to be observed.

Contents

Acknowledgements

Carillion would like to thank the following people for their contribution to this book: Arthur Carter, Derrick Thurlbeck, Steve Olsen and Ralph Need.

Harcourt would like to thank everyone at the Carillion Construction Training Centre in Sunderland for all their help at the photo shoots.

Special thanks to Chris Ledson at Toolbank for supplying some photos. Visit the Toolbank website at www.toolbank.com.

Photos
A1 Pix, p151; Alamy Images/SUNNYPhotography.com, p131 (bottom); Construction Photography, p38, p72 (bottom); Construction Photography/ Xavier de Canto, p153; Corbis, p1, p33, p57, p59 (top), p67, p71, p85, p115, p123, p161, p221; Corbis/Yves Forestier, p213; Corbis/Brigitte Sporrer/zefa, p135; Dreamstime/Jason Stitt, p132; Getty Images/PhotoDisc, p7, p10, p14, p16, p17, p28, p42, p43, p70, p191; Harcourt Ltd, p112 (top); Harcourt Ltd/Chris Honeywell, p58; Harcourt Ltd/Ginny Stroud-Lewis, p60, p61 (top); iStockPhoto/Guy Erwood, p72 (top); Chrissie Martin, p130; Photographers Direct, p131 (top); Photographers Direct/Malcolm Farrow, p129; Shout, p52 (top); Toolbank, p59 (bottom), p61 (bottom), p91 (top left), p95 (bottom), p111 (bottom), p199, p200; Rachael Williams, p2, p128.

All other photos copyright Gareth Boden/Harcourt Ltd.

About this book

This book has been written based on a concept used within Carillion Training Centres for many years. That concept is about providing learners with the necessary information they need to support their studies and at the same time ensuring it is presented in a style which they find both manageable and relevant.

The content of this book has been put together by a team of instructors, each of whom have a wealth of knowledge and experience in both training for NVQs and Technical Certificates and their trade.

This book has been produced to help the learner build a sound knowledge and understanding of all aspects of the NVQ and Technical Certificate requirements associated with their trade. It has also been designed to provide assistance when revising for Technical Certificate end tests and NVQ job knowledge tests.

Each chapter of this book relates closely to a particular unit of the NVQ or Technical Certificate and aims to provide just the right level of information needed to form the required knowledge and understanding of that subject area.

This book provides a basic introduction to the tools, materials and methods of work required to enable you to complete work activities effectively and productively. Upon completion of your studies, this book will remain a valuable source of information and support when carrying out your work activities.

For further information on how the content of this student book matches to the unit requirements of the NVQ and Intermediate Construction Award, please visit www.heinemann.co.uk and follow the FE and Vocational link, followed by the Construction link, where a detailed mapping document is available for download.

Note to tutors: For an On the job for Chapter 7 Preparation of surfaces, please see the Tutor Resource Disk that accompanies this book.

How this book can help you

You will discover a variety of features throughout this book, each of which have been designed and written to increase and improve your knowledge and understanding. These features are:

- **Photographs** – many photographs that appear in this book are specially taken and will help you to follow a step-by-step procedure or identify a tool or material.

- **Illustrations** – clear and colourful drawings will give you more information about a concept or procedure.

- **Definitions** – new or difficult words are picked out in **bold** in the text and defined in the margin.

- **Remember** – key concepts or facts are highlighted in these margin boxes.

- **Find out** – carry out these short activities and gain further information and understanding of a topic area.

- **Did you know?** – interesting facts about the building trade.

- **Safety tips** – follow the guidance in these margin boxes to help you work safely.

- **FAQs** – frequently asked questions appear in all chapters along with informative answers from the experts.

- **On the job scenarios** – read about a real-life situation and answer the questions at the end. What would you do? (Answers can be found in the Tutor Resource Disc that accompanies this book.)

- **End of chapter knowledge checks** – test your understanding and recall of a topic by completing these questions.

- **Glossary** – at the end of this book you will find a comprehensive glossary that defines all the **bold** words and phrases found in the text. A great quick reference tool.

- **Links to useful websites** – any websites referred to in this book can be found at www.heinemann.co.uk/hotlinks. Just enter the express code 3594P to access the links.

chapter 1

The construction industry

OVERVIEW

Construction means creating buildings and services. These might be houses, hospitals, schools, offices, roads, bridges, museums, prisons, train stations, airports, monuments – and anything else you can think of that needs designing and building! What about an Olympic stadium? The 2012 London games will bring a wealth of construction opportunity to the UK and so it is an exciting time to be getting involved.

In the UK, 2.2 million people work in the construction industry – more than in any other – and it is constantly expanding and developing. There are more choices and opportunities than ever before and pay and conditions are improving all the time. Your career doesn't have to end in the UK either – what about taking the skills and experience you are developing abroad? Construction is a career you can take with you wherever you go. There's always going to be something that needs building!

This chapter will cover the following:

- Understanding the industry
- Communication
- Getting involved in the construction industry
- Sources of information and advice.

Understanding the industry

The construction industry is made up of countless companies and businesses that all provide different services and materials. An easy way to divide these companies into categories is according to their size.

- A small company is defined as having between 1 and 49 members of staff.
- A medium company consists of between 50 and 249 members of staff.
- A large company has 250 or more people working for it.

A business might only consist of one member of staff (a sole trader).

The different types of construction work

There are four main types of construction work:

1. New work – this refers to a building that is about to be or has just been built.

2. Maintenance work – this is when an existing building is kept up to an acceptable standard by fixing anything that is damaged so that it does not fall into disrepair.

3. Refurbishment/renovation work – this generally refers to an existing building that has fallen into a state of disrepair and is then brought up to standard by repair. It also refers to an existing building that is to be used for a different purpose, for example, changing an old bank into a pub.

4. Restoration work – this refers to an existing building that has fallen into a state of disrepair and is then brought back to its original condition or use.

New work is just one type of construction area

Find out

Think of an example of a small, medium and large construction company. Do you know of any construction companies that have only one member of staff?

These four types of work can fall into one of two categories depending upon who is paying for the work:

1. Public – the government pays for the work, as is the case with most schools and hospitals etc.

2. Private – work is paid for by a private client and can range from extensions on existing houses to new houses or buildings.

Job and careers

Jobs and careers in the construction industry fall mainly into one of four categories:

1. building

2. civil engineering

3. electrical engineering

4. mechanical engineering.

Building involves the physical construction (making) of a structure. It also involves the maintenance, restoration and refurbishment of structures.

Civil engineering involves the construction and maintenance of work such as roads, railways, bridges etc.

Electrical engineering involves the installation and maintenance of electrical systems and devices such as lights, power sockets and electrical appliances etc.

Mechanical engineering involves the installation and maintenance of things such as heating, ventilation and lifts.

The category that is the most relevant to your course is building.

Painters and decorators are building craft workers

Job types

The construction industry employs people in four specific areas:

1. professionals
2. technicians
3. building craft workers
4. building operatives.

Professionals

Professionals are generally of graduate level (i.e. people who have a degree from a university) and may have one of the following types of job in the construction industry:

- architect – someone who designs and draws the building or structure
- structural engineer – someone who oversees the strength and structure of the building
- surveyor – someone who checks the land for suitability to build on
- service engineer – someone who plans the services needed within the building, for example, gas, electricity and water supplies.

Technicians

Technicians link professional workers with craft workers and are made up of the following people:

- architectural technician – someone who looks at the architect's information and makes drawings that can be used by the builder
- building technician – someone who is responsible for estimating the cost of the work and materials and general site management
- quantity surveyor – someone who calculates ongoing costs and payment for work done.

Building craft workers

Building craft workers are the skilled people who work with materials to physically construct the building. The following jobs fall into this category:

- carpenter or joiner – someone who works with wood but also other construction materials such as plastic and iron. A carpenter primarily works on site while a joiner usually works off site, producing components such as windows, stairs, doors, kitchens, and **trusses**, which the carpenter then fits into the building

- bricklayer – someone who works with bricks, blocks and cement to build the structure of the building

- plasterer – someone who adds finish to the internal walls and ceilings by applying a **plaster skim**. They also make and fix plaster **covings** and plaster decorations

- painter and decorator – someone who uses paint and paper to decorate the internal plaster and timberwork such as walls, ceilings, windows and doors, as well as **architraves** and **skirting**

- electrician – someone who fits all electrical systems and fittings within a building, including power supplies, lights and power sockets

- plumber – someone who fits all water services within a building, including sinks, boilers, water tanks, radiators, toilets and baths. The plumber also deals with lead work and rainwater fittings such as guttering

- slater and tiler – someone who fits tiles on to the roof of a building, ensuring that the building is watertight

- woodworking machinist – someone who works in a machine shop, converting timber into joinery components such as window sections, spindles for stairs, architraves and skirting boards, amongst other things. They use a variety of machines such as lathes, bench saws, planers and sanders.

Definition

Trusses – prefabricated components of a roof which spread the load of a roof over the outer walls and form its shape

Plaster skim – a thin layer of plaster that is put on to walls to give a smooth and even finish

Covings – a decorative moulding that is fitted at the top of a wall where it meets the ceiling

Architraves – a decorative moulding, usually made from timber, that is fitted around door and window frames to hide the gap between the frame and the wall

Skirting – a decorative moulding that is fitted at the bottom of a wall to hide the gap between the wall and the floor

Building operatives

There are two different building operatives working on a construction site.

1. Specialist building operative – someone who carries out specialist operations such as dry wall lining, asphalting, scaffolding, floor and wall tiling and glazing.

2. General building operative – someone who carries out non-specialist operations such as kerb laying, concreting, path laying and drainage. These operatives also support other craft workers and do general labouring. They use a variety of hand tools and power tools as well as **plant**, such as dumper trucks and JCBs.

The building team

Constructing a building or structure is a huge task that needs to be done by a team of people who all need to work together towards the same goal. The team of people is often known as the building team and is made up of the following people.

Clients

The client is the person who requires the building or refurbishment. This person is the most important person in the building team because they finance the project fully and without the client there is no work. The client can be a single person or a large organisation.

Architect

The architect works closely with the client, interpreting their requirements to produce contract documents that enable the client's wishes to be realised.

Clerk of works

Selected by the architect or client to oversee the actual building process, the clerk of works ensures that construction sticks to agreed deadlines. They also monitor the quality of workmanship.

Definition

Plant – industrial machinery

Local Authority

The Local Authority is responsible for ensuring that construction projects meet relevant planning and building legislation. Planning and building control officers approve and inspect building work.

Quantity surveyor

The quantity surveyor works closely with the architect and client, acting as an accountant for the job. They are responsible for the ongoing evaluation of cost and interim payments from the client, establishing whether or not the contract is on budget. The quantity surveyor will prepare and sign off final accounts when the contract is complete.

The building team is made up of many different people

Specialist engineers

Specialist engineers assist the architect in specialist areas, such as civil engineering, structural engineering and service engineering.

Health and safety inspectors

Employed by the Health and Safety Executive (HSE), health and safety inspectors ensure that the building contractor fully implements and complies with government health and safety legislation. For more information on health and safety in the construction industry, see Chapter 2 (page 33).

Building contractors

The building contractors agree to carry out building work for the client. Contractors will employ the required workforce based on the size of the contract.

Estimator

The estimator works with the contractor on the cost of carrying out the building contract, listing each item in the bill of quantities (e.g. materials, labour and plant). They calculate the overall cost for the contractor to complete the contract, including further costs as overheads, such as site offices, management administration and pay, not forgetting profit.

Site agent

The site agent works for the building contractor and is responsible for the day-to-day running of the site such as organising deliveries etc.

Suppliers

The suppliers work with the contractor and estimator to arrange the materials that are needed on site and ensure that they are delivered on time and in good condition.

General foreman

The general foreman works for the site manager and is responsible for co-ordinating the work of the ganger (see below), craft foreman and subcontractors. They may also be responsible for the hiring and firing of site operatives. The general foreman also liaises with the clerk of works.

Craft foreman

The craft foreman works for the general foreman organising and supervising the work of particular crafts. For example, the carpentry craft foreman will be responsible for all carpenters on site.

Ganger

The ganger supervises the general building operatives.

Chargehand

The chargehand is normally employed only on large building projects, being responsible for various craftsmen and working with joiners, bricklayers, and plasterers.

Operatives

Operatives are the workers who carry out the building work, and are divided into three subsections:

1. Craft operatives are skilled tradesman such as joiners, plasterers, bricklayers.

2. Building operatives include general building operatives who are responsible for drain laying, mixing concrete, unloading materials and keeping the site clean.

3. Specialist operatives include tilers, pavers, glaziers, scaffolders and plant operators.

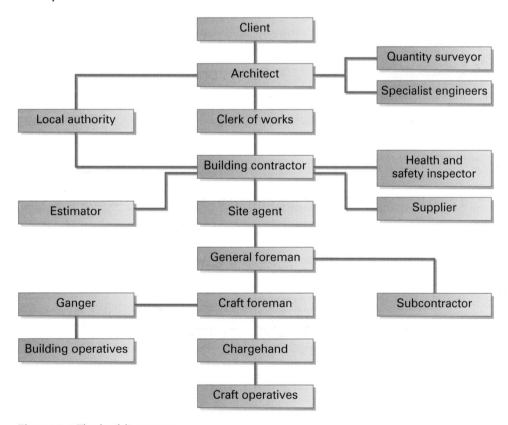

Figure 1.1 The building team

The different types of building

There are of course lots of very different types of building, but the main types are:

- residential – houses and flats etc.

- commercial – shops and supermarkets etc.

- industrial – warehouses and factories etc.

A low rise residential building

These types of building can be further broken down by the height or number of storeys that they have (one storey being the level from floor to ceiling):

- low rise – a building with one to three storeys

- medium rise – a building with four to seven storeys

- high rise – a building with seven storeys or more.

Buildings can also be categorised according to the number of other buildings they are attached to:

- detached – a building that stands alone and is not connected to any other building

- semi-detached – a building that is joined to one other building and shares a dividing wall, called a party wall

- terraced – a row of three or more buildings that are joined together, of which the inner buildings share two party walls.

Building requirements

Every building must meet the minimum requirements of the *Building Regulations*, which were first introduced in 1961 and then updated in 1985. The purpose of building regulations is to ensure that safe and healthy buildings are constructed for the public and that **conservation** is taken into account when they are being constructed. Building regulations enforce a minimum standard of building work and ensure that the materials used are of a good standard and fit for purpose.

Definition

Conservation – preservation of the environment and wildlife

What makes a good building?

When a building is designed, there are certain things that need to be taken into consideration, such as:

- security
- safety
- privacy
- warmth
- light
- ventilation.

A well designed building will meet the minimum standards for all of the considerations above and will also be built in line with building regulations.

Identifying the different parts of a building

All buildings consist of the following two main parts:

1. the substructure
2. the superstructure.

The substructure consists of all building work below the ground level, including the foundations, up to the **damp proof course**. The purpose of the substructure is to spread the load of the building.

The superstructure consists of all the building work above the substructure and its purpose is to provide shelter and divide space.

The things that make up the substructure or superstructure can be divided into four different sections:

1. Primary elements – these include the main parts of the building that provide support, protection, floor-to-floor access and the division of space. Examples of primary elements are foundations, walls, floors, roofs and stairs.

2. Secondary elements – these include the non-essential and non-load bearing parts that are used to close off openings or to provide a finish. Examples of secondary elements are doors, windows, skirting and architraves.

3. Finishing elements – these include the final parts required to complete a component and can be superficial or necessary to complete the job. Examples of finishing elements are paint, wallpaper, plaster or face brickwork.

4. Services – these are the electrical, mechanical and specialist installations that are normally piped or wired into the building. Examples of services are running water and electricity.

Figure 1.2 The four elements of a building

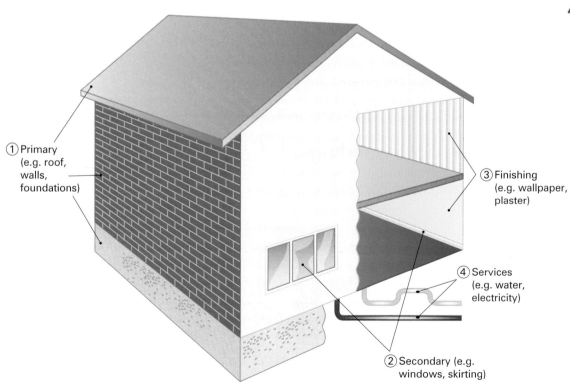

① Primary (e.g. roof, walls, foundations)

③ Finishing (e.g. wallpaper, plaster)

④ Services (e.g. water, electricity)

② Secondary (e.g. windows, skirting)

Communication

Communication, in the simplest of terms, is a way or means of passing on information from one person to another. Communication is very important in all areas of life and we often do it without even thinking about it. You will need to communicate well when you are at work, no matter what job you do. What would happen if someone couldn't understand something you had written or said? If we don't communicate well, how will other people know what we want or need and how will we know what other people want?

Companies that do not establish good methods of communicating with their workforce or with other companies, will not function properly and will end up with bad working relationships. Good working relationships can *only* be achieved with co-operation and good communication.

Methods of communication

There are many different ways of communicating with others and they all generally fit into one of these three categories:

1. speaking (verbal communication), for example talking face to face or over the telephone

2. writing, for example sending a letter or taking a message

3. body language, for example the way we stand or our facial expressions.

Each method of communicating has good points (advantages) and bad points (disadvantages).

Verbal communication

Verbal communication is the most common method we use to communicate with each other. If two people don't speak the same language or if someone speaks very quietly or not very clearly, verbal communication cannot be effective. Working in the construction industry you may communicate verbally with other people face to face, over the telephone or by radio/walkie-talkie.

Verbal communication is probably the method you will use most

Advantages

Verbal communication is instant, easy and can be repeated or rephrased until the message is understood.

Disadvantages

Verbal communication can be easily forgotten as there is no physical evidence of the message. Because of this it can be easily changed if passed to other people. Someone's accent or use of slang language can sometimes make it difficult to understand what they are saying.

Written communication

Written communication can take the form of letters, faxes, messages, notes, instruction leaflets, text messages, drawings and emails, amongst others.

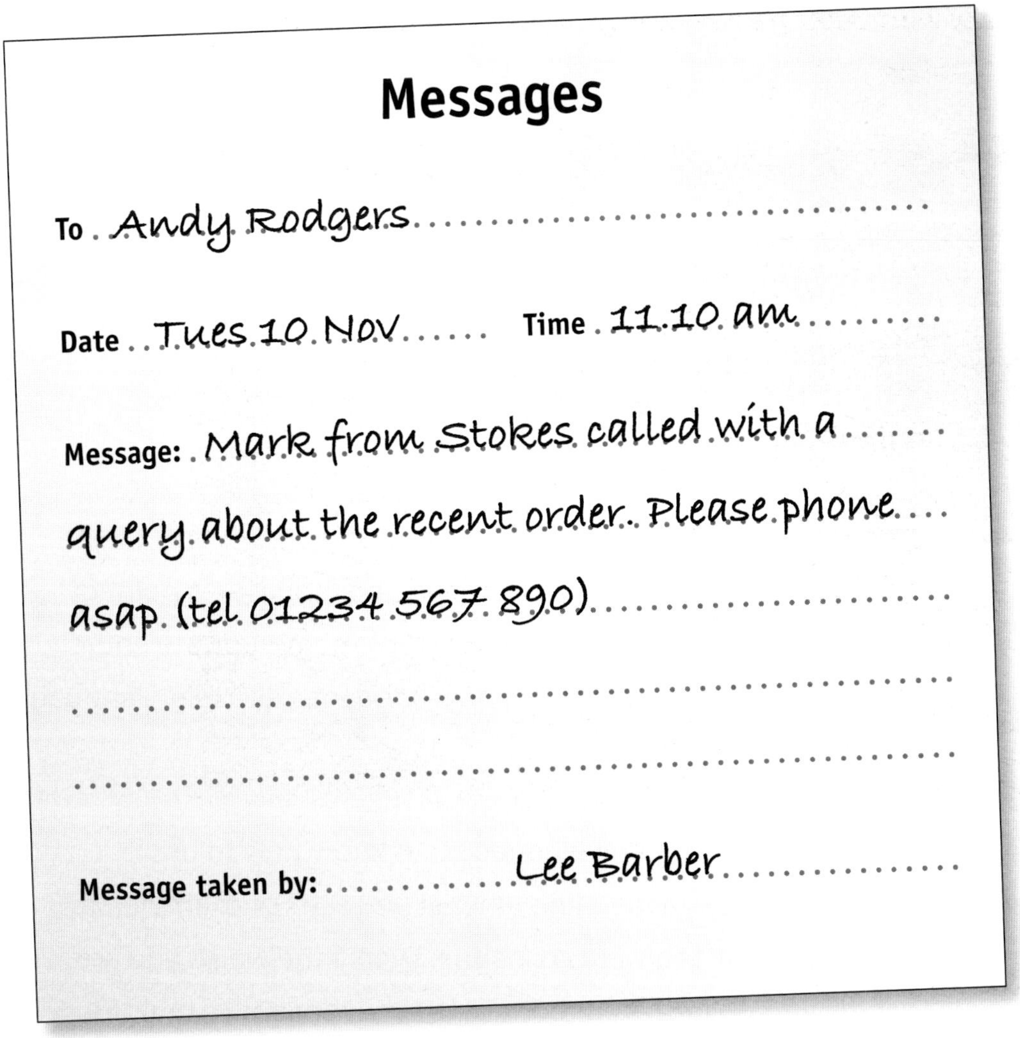

Messages

To Andy Rodgers.....................................

Date ..Tues.10.Nov...... Time .11.10.am..........

Message: .Mark.from.Stokes.called.with.a.......
query.about.the.recent.order..Please.phone....
asap.(tel.01234.567.890)....................
....
....

Message taken by: ....Lee Barber...............

Figure 1.3 A message is a form of written communication

Advantages

There is physical evidence of the communication and the message can be passed on to another person without it being changed. It can also be read again if it is not understood.

Disadvantages

Written communication takes longer to arrive and understand than verbal communication and body language. It can also be misunderstood or lost. If it is handwritten, the reader may not be able to read the writing if it is messy.

Try to be aware of your body language

Body language

It is said that, when we are talking to someone face to face, only 10 per cent of the communication is verbal. The rest of the communication is body language and facial expression. This form of communication can be as simple as the shaking of a head from left to right to mean 'no' or as complex as the way someone's face changes when they are happy or sad or the signs given in body language when someone is lying.

We often use hand gestures as well as words to get across what we are saying, to emphasise a point or give a direction. Some people communicate entirely through a form of body language called sign language.

Advantages

If you are aware of your own body language and know how to use it effectively, you can add extra meaning to what you say. For example, say you are talking to a client or a work colleague. Even if the words you are using are friendly and polite, if your body language is negative or unfriendly, the message that you are giving out could be misunderstood. By simply maintaining eye contact, smiling and not folding your arms, you have made sure that the person you are communicating with has not got a mixed or confusing message.

Body language is quick and effective. A wave from a distance can pass on a greeting without being close, and using hand signals to direct a lorry or a load from a crane is instant and doesn't require any equipment such as radios.

Disadvantages

Some gestures can be misunderstood, especially if they are given from very far away, and gestures that have one meaning in one country or culture can have a completely different meaning in another.

Which type of communication should I use?

Of the many different types of communication, the type you should use will depend upon the situation. If someone needs to be told something formally, then written communication is generally the best way. If the message is informal, then verbal communication is usually acceptable.

The way that you communicate will also be affected by who it is you are communicating with. You should of course always communicate in a polite and respectful manner with anyone you have contact with, but you need to also be aware of the need to sometimes alter the style of your communication. For example, when talking to a friend, it may be fine to talk in a very informal way and use slang language, but in a work situation with a client or a colleague, it is best to alter your communication to a more formal style in order to show professionalism. In the same way, it may be fine to leave a message or send a text to a friend that says 'C U @ 8 4 work', but if you wrote this down for a work colleague or a client to read, it would not look very professional and they may not understand it.

You will work with people from other trades

Communicating with other trades

Communicating with other trades is vital because they need to know what you are doing and when, and you need to know the same information from them. Poor communication can lead to delays and mistakes, which can both be costly. It is quite possible for poor communication to result in work having to be stopped or redone. Say you are decorating a room in a new building. You are just about to finish when you find out that the electrician, plumber and carpenter have to finish off some work in the room. This information didn't reach you and now the decorating will have to be done again once the other work has been finished. What a waste of time and money. A situation like this can be avoided with good communication between the trades.

Common methods of communicating in the construction industry

A career in construction means that you will often have to use written documents such as drawings, specifications and schedules. These documents can be very large and seem very complicated but, if you understand what they are used for and how they work, using such documents will soon become second nature.

Drawings

Drawings are done by the architect and are used to pass on the client's wishes to the building contractor. Drawings are usually done to scale, whereby the drawing is drawn to a certain scale because it would be impossible to draw a full-sized version of the project. A common scale is 1:10, which means that a line 10 mm long on the drawing represents 100 mm in real life. Drawings often contain symbols instead of written words to get the maximum amount of information across without cluttering the page.

Specifications

Specifications accompany a drawing and give you the sizes that are not available on the drawing, as well as telling you the type of material to be used and the quality that the work has to be finished to.

Schedules

A schedule is a list of repeated design information used on big building sites when there are several types of similar room or house. For example, a schedule will tell you what type of door must be used and where. Another form of schedule used on building sites contains a detailed list of dates by which work must be carried out and materials delivered etc.

Other documents

As well as drawings, specifications and schedules there are some other important types of documents you will come across that are not specifically about the building or structure you are working on. Rather, they are about your day-to-day tasks and your job. We will now look at a selection of these documents.

Timesheet

A timesheet is used to record the hours you have worked and where the work was carried out. Failure to complete your timesheet accurately and submit it on time may result in a loss of wages.

P. Gresford Building Contractors

Timesheet _____

Employee _____ **Project/site** _____

Date	Job no.	Start time	Finish time	Total time	Travel time	Expenses
M						
Tu						
W						
Th						
F						
Sa						
Su						
Totals						

Employee's signature _____

Supervisor's signature _____

Date _____

Figure 1.4 A typical timesheet

P. Greford Building Contractors

Jobsheet

Customer   Chris MacFarlane

Address   1 High Street
Any Town
Any County

Work to be carried out

Paint rendering at front of building

Special conditions/instructions

3 × coats of masonry paint

Figure 1.5 A typical jobsheet

Jobsheet/Day worksheet

A jobsheet is also used to record work to be done. A day worksheet is used to record work done that wasn't originally planned and shown in the jobsheet.

P. Gresford Building Contractors

Day worksheet

Customer _____   Date _____

Description of work being carried out _____

_____

_____

Labour	Craft	Hours	Gross rate	TOTALS
Materials	Quantity	Rate	% addition	
Plant	Hours	Rate	% addition	

Comments

Signed _____   Date _____

Site manager/foreman signature _____

Figure 1.6 A typical day worksheet

Requisition form

A requisition form (also known as an order form) is used when you require plant, materials or equipment. Once you have worked out what you need and how much of it you need, a requisition form can then be filled in and sent to the relevant supplier.

Remember

Make sure you have all the tools and equipment you need before you go to do a job. You will need to plan ahead and fill in a requisition form early!

P. Gresford Building Contractors

Requisition form

Supplier _____

_____

Tel no. _____

Fax no. _____

Contract/Delivery address/Invoice address

_____

_____

Tel no. _____

Fax no. _____

Order no. _____

Serial no. _____

Contact _____

Our ref _____

Statements/applications

for payments to be sent to

_____

_____

_____

Item no.	Quantity	Unit	Description	Unit price	Amount

Total £ _____

Payment terms _____

Originated by _____

Authorised by _____

Date _____

Figure 1.7 A typical requisition form (order form)

Delivery note

A delivery note is sent by a supplier along with an order. It lists the materials delivered and the quantity. If you receive a delivery, you must check the delivery note against the tools, equipment or materials delivered. If everything matches, then you can sign the note. If anything is missing or damaged, you should not sign the note and must inform your supervisor.

Delivery note

Bailey & Sons Ltd

Building materials supplier

Tel: 01234 567890

Your ref: AB00671

Our ref: CT020

Date: 17 Jul 2006

Order no: 67440387

Invoice address:
Carillion Training Centre,
Deptford Terrace, Sunderland

Delivery address:
Same as invoice

Description of goods	Quantity	Catalogue no.
5l matt emulsion (white)	5	TL5W

Comments:
Date and time of receiving goods:
Name of recipient (caps):
Signature:

Figure 1.8 A typical delivery note

Work programme

A work programme is a method of showing very easily what work is being carried out on a building and when. Used by many site agents or supervisors, a work programme is a bar chart that lists the tasks that need to be done down the left side and shows a timeline across the top (see Figure 1.9). A work programme is used to make sure that the relevant trade is on site at the correct time and that materials are delivered when needed. A site agent or supervisor can quickly tell from looking at the chart if work is keeping to schedule or falling behind.

Activity	Time in days						
	1	2	3	4	5	6	7
A	■						
B	■	■	■				
C		■	■				
D			■	■	■		
E		■	■	■	■	■	■
F				■	■	■	■
G						■	■

Figure 1.9 A work programme

Getting involved in the construction industry

There are many ways of entering the construction industry, but the most common way is as an apprentice.

Apprenticeships

You can become an apprentice by:

1. Being employed directly by a construction company who will send you to college.

2. Being employed by a training provider, such as Carillion, which combines construction training with practical work experience.

An apprenticeship will give you on-the-job training and experience

On 1 August 2002, the construction industry introduced a mandatory induction programme for all apprentices joining the industry. The programme has four distinct areas:

1. apprenticeship framework requirements

2. the construction industry

3. employment

4. health and safety.

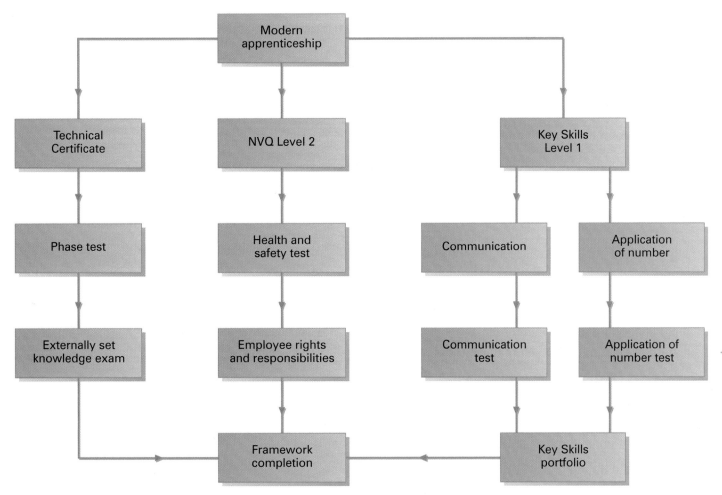

Figure 1.10 Apprenticeship framework

Apprenticeship frameworks are based on a number of components designed to prepare people for work in a particular construction occupation.

Construction frameworks are made up of the following mandatory components:

- NVQs
- technical certificates (construction awards)
- key skills.

However, certain trades require additional components. Bricklaying, for example, requires abrasive wheels certification.

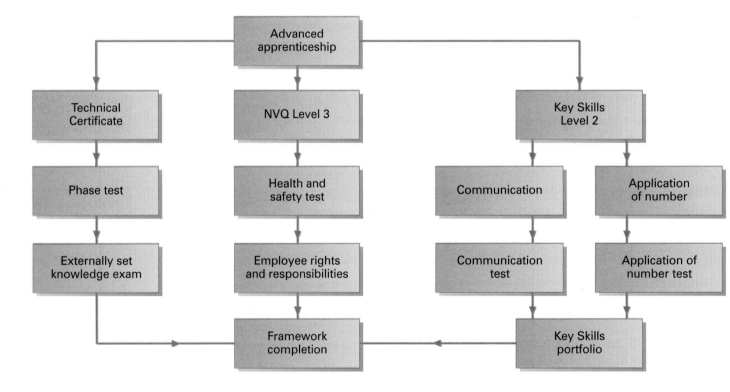

Figure 1.11 Advanced apprenticeship framework

National Vocational Qualifications (NVQs)

NVQs are available to anyone, with no restrictions on age, length or type of training, although learners below a certain age can only perform certain tasks. There are different levels of NVQ (e.g. 1, 2 , 3), which in turn are broken down into units of competence. NVQs are not like traditional examinations in which someone sits an exam paper. An NVQ is a 'doing' qualification, which means it lets the industry know that you have the knowledge, skills and ability to actually 'do' something.

The Construction Industry Training Board (CITB) is the national training organisation for construction in the UK and is responsible for setting training standards. NVQs are made up of both mandatory and optional units and the number of units that you need to complete for an NVQ depends on the level and the occupation.

NVQs are assessed in the workplace, and several types of evidence are used:

- Witness testimony consists of evidence provided by various individuals who have first-hand knowledge of your work and performance relating to the NVQ. Work colleagues, supervisors and even customers can provide evidence of your performance.

- Your natural performance can be observed a number of times in the workplace while carrying out work-related activities.

- The use of historical evidence means that you can use evidence from past achievements or experience, if it is directly related to the NVQ.

- Assignments or projects can be used to assess your knowledge and understanding of a subject.

- Photographic evidence showing you performing various tasks in the workplace can be used, providing it is authenticated by your supervisor.

Technical certificates

Technical certificates are often related to NVQs. A certificate provides evidence that you have the underpinning knowledge and understanding required to complete a particular task. An off-the-job training programme, either in a college or with a training provider, may deliver technical certificates. You generally have to sit an end-of-programme exam to achieve the full certificate.

Key skills

Some students have key skills development needs, so learners and apprentices must achieve key skills at Level 1 or 2 in both Communications and Application of number. Key skills are signposted in each level of the NVQ and are assessed independently, so you will need to be released from your training to attend a key skills test.

Employment

Conditions of employment are controlled by legislation and regulations. The Department of Trade and Industry (DTI) publishes most of this legislation. To find out more about your working rights, visit the DTI website. A quick link has been made available at www.heinemann.co.uk/hotlinks – just enter the express code 3594P.

The main pieces of legislation that will apply to you are:

- The Employment Act 2002 which gives extra rights to working parents and gives new guidance on resolving disputes, amongst other things.

- The Employment Relations Act 1999 covers areas such as trade union membership and disciplinary and grievance proceedings.

The Race Relations Act protects people of all skin colours, races and nationalities

- The Employment Rights Act 1996 details the rights an employee has by law, including the right to have time off work and the right to be given notice if being dismissed.

- The Sex Discrimination Acts of 1975 and 1986 state that it is illegal for an employee to be treated less favourably because of their sex, for example, paying a man more than a woman or offering a woman more holiday than a man, even though they do the same job.

- The Race Relations Act 1976 states that it is against the law for someone to be treated less favourably because of their skin colour, race, nationality or ethnic origin.

- The Disability Discrimination Act 1995 makes it illegal for someone to be treated less favourably just because they have a physical or mental disability.

- The National Minimum Wage Act 1998 makes sure that everyone in the UK is paid a minimum amount. How much you must be paid depends on how old you are and whether or not you are on an Apprenticeship Scheme. The national minimum wage is periodically assessed and increased so it is a good idea to make sure you know what it is. At the time of writing, under 18s and those on Apprenticeship Schemes do not qualify for the minimum wage. For those aged 18–21, the minimum wage is £4.25 per hour and for adult workers aged 22 or over, the minimum wage is £5.05 per hour.

Find out

What is the national minimum wage at the moment? You can find out from lots of different places, including the DTI website. You can find a link to the site at www.heinemann.co.uk/hotlinks – just enter the express code 3594P

Contract of employment

Within two months of starting a new job, your employer must give you a contract of employment. This will tell you the terms of your employment and should include the following information:

- job title
- place of work
- hours of work
- rates of pay
- holiday pay
- overtime rates
- statutory sick pay
- pension scheme
- discipline procedure
- termination of employment
- dispute procedure.

If you have any questions about information contained within your contract of employment, you should talk to your supervisor before you sign it.

When you start a new job, you should also receive a copy of the safety policy and an employee handbook containing details of the general policy, procedures and disciplinary rules.

Discrimination in the workplace

Discrimination means treating someone unjustly, and in the workplace it can range from bullying, intimidation or harassment to paying someone less money or not giving them a job. Discriminating against people within the working environment is against the law. This includes discrimination on the grounds of:

- sex, gender or sexual orientation
- race, colour, nationality or ethnic origin
- religious beliefs
- disability.

The law states that employment, training and promotion should be open to all employees regardless of any of the above. Pay should be equal for men and women if they are required to do the same job.

Men and women must be treated equally at work

Sources of information and advice

There are many places you can go to get information and advice about a career in the construction industry. If you are already studying, you can speak to your tutor, your school or college careers advisor or you can get in touch with Connexions for careers advice especially for young people. Visit www.heinemann.co.uk/hotlinks and enter the express code 3594P for a link to Connexions' website. You can also find their telephone number in your local phonebook.

Organisations such as those listed below are very good sources of careers advice specific to the construction industry.

- CITB (Construction Industry Training Board) – the industry's national training organisation
- City and Guilds – a provider of recognised vocational qualifications
- The Chartered Institute of Building Services Engineers
- The Institute of Civil Engineers
- Trade unions such as GMB (Britain's General Union), UCATT (Union of Construction, Allied Trades and Technicians), UNISON (the public services union), Amicus (the manufacturing union, previously MSF)

Links to all these organisations' websites can be found by visiting www.heinemann.co.uk/hotlinks and entering the express code 3594P.

FAQ

Why do I need to learn about different trades?

It is very important that you have some basic knowledge of what other trades do. This is because you will often work with people from other trades and their work will affect yours and vice versa.

What options do I have once I have gained my NVQ Level 2 qualification?

Once you are qualified, there is a wide range of career opportunities available to you. For example, you could progress from a tradesman to a foreman and then to a site agent. There may also be the opportunity to become a clerk of works, an architect or a college lecturer. Some tradesmen are happy to continue as tradesmen and some start up their own businesses.

Knowledge check

1. How many members of staff are there in a small company, a medium company and a large company?

2. Give an example of a public construction project. Who pays for public work?

3. Name a job in each of the four construction employment areas: professional; technician; building craft worker; building operative.

4. Why is the client the most important member of the building team?

5. Explain the meaning of the following building types: a) residential, b) low rise, and c) semi-detached.

6. What is the substructure of a building?

7. What are the three different methods of communication?

8. What information might a schedule give you?

9. What does NVQ stand for?

10. What information must be in your contract of employment?

chapter 2

Health and safety

OVERVIEW

Every year in the construction industry over 100 people are killed and thousands more are seriously injured as a result of the work that they do. There are thousands more who suffer from health problems, such as dermatitis, asbestosis, industrial asthma, vibration white finger and deafness. You can therefore see why learning as much as you can about health and safety is very important.

This chapter will cover:

- Health and safety legislation
- Health and welfare in the construction industry
- Manual handling
- Fire and fire-fighting equipment
- Safety signs
- Personal protective equipment (PPE)
- Reporting accidents
- Risk assessment.

Health and safety legislation

While you are at work, in whatever location or environment that may be (e.g. on a building site or in a client's home), you need to be aware of some important laws that are there to protect you from harm. The laws state how you should be protected and what your **employer** has to do to keep you safe, i.e. their responsibilities.

Health and safety legislation not only protects you, but also states what your responsibilities are in order to keep others safe. It is very important that you follow any guidance given to you regarding health and safety and that you know what your responsibilities are.

What is legislation?

The word legislation generally refers to a law that is made in Parliament and is often called an act. For our purposes, health and safety acts state what should and shouldn't be done by employers and employees in order to keep work places safe. If an employer or an employee does something they shouldn't, or just as importantly, doesn't do something they should, they could face paying a large fine or even a prison sentence.

Health and safety legislation you need to be aware of

There are a lot of different pieces of legislation and regulations that affect the construction industry. Over the next few pages are just a few of those that you need to be aware of. Some of these are dealt with in more detail later on in this chapter.

Health and Safety at Work Act 1974

The Health and Safety at Work Act 1974 applies to all places of work, not just construction environments. It not only protects employers and employees but also any member of the public who might be affected by the work being done. The act outlines what must be done by employers and employees to ensure that the work they do is safe.

The main objectives of the Health and Safety at Work Act are:

- To ensure the health, safety and welfare of all persons at work.

- To protect the general public from work activities.

- To control the use, handling, storage and transportation of explosives and highly flammable substances.

- To control the release of **noxious** or offensive substances into the atmosphere.

The Health and Safety at Work Act is **enforced** by the **Health and Safety Executive** (HSE). HSE inspectors have the power to:

- Enter any premises to carry out investigations.

- Take statements and check records.

- Demand seizure, dismantle, neutralise or destroy anything that is likely to cause immediate serious injury.

- Issue an improvement notice, which gives a company a certain amount of time to sort out a health and safety problem.

- Issue a prohibition notice, which stops all work until the situation is safe.

- Give guidance and advice on health and safety matters.

- **Prosecute** people who break the law, including employers, employees, self-employed manufacturers and suppliers.

As we learnt at the beginning of this chapter, employers and employees have certain responsibilities under health and safety legislation. These are often referred to as 'duties' and are things that should or shouldn't be done by law. If you do not carry out your duties, you are breaking the law and you could be prosecuted.

Definition

Noxious – harmful or poisonous

Find out

Will you be working with any highly flammable, explosive or noxious substances? What are they?

Definition

Enforced – making sure a law is obeyed

Prosecute – to accuse someone of committing a crime, which usually results in being taken to court and, if found guilty, being punished

Duties of the employer

Under the Health and Safety at Work Act employers must:

- provide a safe entrance and exit to the workplace

- provide a safe place to work

- provide and maintain safe machinery and equipment

- provide employees with the necessary training to be able to do their job safely

- have a written safety policy

- ensure safe handling, transportation and storage of machinery, equipment and materials

- provide personal protective equipment (PPE)

- involve trade union safety representatives, where appointed, in all matters relating to health and safety.

You have a legal duty to work safely at all times

Duties of the employee

Under the Health and Safety at Work Act employees must:

- take care at all times and ensure that they do not put themselves or others at risk by their actions

- co-operate with employers in regard to health and safety

- use any equipment and safeguards provided by their employer

- not misuse or interfere with anything that is provided for their safety.

Control of Substances Hazardous to Health Regulations 2002 (COSHH)

The COSHH regulations state how employees and employers should work with, handle, move and dispose safely of potentially dangerous substances. A substance hazardous to health is anything that might negatively affect your health, for example:

- dust or small particles from things like bricks and wood and fumes from chemicals
- chemicals in things like paint, **adhesives** and cement
- explosive or flammable chemicals or material.

The main aim of the COSHH regulations is to ensure that any risks due to working with hazardous substances or being exposed to them are assessed. Action must then be taken to eliminate or control the risks.

There are three different ways in which hazardous substances can enter the body:

1. Inhalation – breathing in the dangerous substance
2. Absorption – when the hazardous substance enters the body through the skin
3. Ingestion – taking in the hazardous substance through the mouth.

The COSHH regulations are as follows:

1. You should know exactly what products and substances you are using. You should be told this information by your employer.
2. Any hazards to health from using a substance or being exposed to it must be assessed by your employer.
3. If a substance is associated with any hazards to health, your employer must eliminate or control the hazard by either using a different substance or by making sure the substance is used according to guidelines (i.e. used outside or only used for short periods of time). Your

Definition

Adhesive – glue

Find out

Will you be working with any substances hazardous to health? What precautions and safety measures do you think should be taken for each?

Remember

It is not always possible to see a harmful substance so, if you are given any PPE or instructions about how to use/move/dispose of something, use them. Don't think that just because you can't see a hazardous substance, it isn't there

employer must also provide you with appropriate PPE and make sure that all possible precautions are taken.

4. Your employer must ensure that people are properly trained and informed of any hazards. All staff should be trained to recognise identifiable hazards and should know the correct precautions to take.

5. In order to make sure precautions are up to date, your employer has to monitor all tasks and change any control methods when required.

6. In case anyone ever needs to know what happened in the past, a record of all substances used by employees must be kept.

Safety tip

If you come across a substance that you are unsure about, do not use it. Report it to your supervisor as soon as possible

Provision and Use of Work Equipment Regulations 1998 (PUWER)

The PUWER regulations cover all working equipment such as tools and machinery. Under the PUWER regulations, employers must make sure that any tools and equipment they provide are:

- suitable for the job

- maintained (serviced and repaired)

- inspected (a regular check that ensures the piece of equipment and its parts are still in good working condition).

Under PUWER, all tools and equipment must be regularly serviced and repaired

Employers also have to make sure that any risk of harm from using the equipment has been identified and all precautions and safety measures have been taken. Employers must also ensure that anyone who uses the equipment has been properly trained and instructed in how to do so.

The Manual Handling Operations Regulations 1992

These regulations cover all work activities in which a person does the lifting instead of a machine. The correct and safe way to lift, which reduces the risk of injury, is covered later on in this chapter (see page 45).

The Control of Noise at Work Regulations 2005

In the course of your career in construction, it is likely that you will be at some time working in a noisy environment. The Control of Noise at Work Regulations are there to protect you against the consequences of being exposed to high levels of noise, which can lead to permanent hearing damage.

Damage to hearing can be caused by:

* the volume of noise (measured in decibels)
* the length of time exposed to the noise (over a day, over a lifetime etc.).

The regulations give guidance on the maximum period of time someone can be safely exposed to a decibel level, and your employer has to follow it.

If you have access to the internet, you might wish to visit the Health and Safety Executive website and find out what it is like to have hearing loss caused by long-term exposure to noise. A link to the web page has been made available at www.heinemann.co.uk/hotlinks – just enter the express code 3594P.

The Work at Height Regulations 2005

It is not at all unusual for a construction worker to carry out their everyday job high up off the ground, for example, on scaffolding, on a ladder, or on the roof of a building. The Work at Height Regulations make sure that your employer does all that they can to reduce the risk of injury or death from working at height. Your employer has a duty to:

- avoid work at height where possible
- use equipment that will prevent falls
- use equipment and other methods that will minimise the distance and consequences of a fall.

As an employee, under the regulations you must follow any training that has been given to you, report any hazards to your supervisor and use any safety equipment that is made available to you.

The Electricity at Work Regulations 1989

The Electricity at Work Regulations cover any work that involves the use of electricity or electrical equipment. Your employer has a duty to make sure that electrical systems you may come into contact with are safe and regularly maintained. They also have to make sure that they have done everything the law states to reduce the risk of an employee coming into contact with a live electrical current.

The Personal Protective Equipment at Work Regulations 1992

There are certain situations in which you will need to wear personal protective equipment (PPE). The Personal Protective Equipment at Work Regulations details the different types of PPE that are available and states when they should be worn. Your employer has to ensure appropriate PPE is available for certain tasks (e.g. gloves when working with solvents, face masks when cutting bricks, safety goggles when using a circular saw).

The different types of PPE available are covered in more detail later on in this chapter (see page 57).

Reporting of Injuries, Diseases and Dangerous Occurrences Regulations 1995 (RIDDOR)

Employers have duties under RIDDOR to report accidents, diseases or dangerous occurrences. This information is used by the HSE to identify where and how risk arises and to investigate serious accidents.

Several other regulations exist which cover very specific things such as asbestos, pressure equipment and lead paint. If you want to find out more about these regulations, or any others, ask your tutor or employer for more information or visit the Health and Safety Executive website (go to www.heinemann.co.uk/hotlinks and enter the express code 3594P for a quick link).

Health and welfare in the construction industry

Jobs in the construction industry have one of the highest injury and accident rates and as a worker you will be at constant risk unless you adopt a good health and safety attitude. By following the rules and regulations set out to protect you and by taking reasonable care of yourself and others, you will become a safe worker and thus reduce the chance of any injuries or accidents.

The most common risks to a construction worker

What do you think these might be? Think about the construction industry you are working in and the hazards and risks that exist.

The most common health and safety risks a construction worker faces are:

- accidents
- ill health.

Accidents

We often hear the saying 'accidents will happen', but when working in the construction industry, we should not accept that accidents just happen

Remember

Health and safety laws are there to protect you and other people. If you take shortcuts or ignore the rules, you are placing yourself and others at serious risk sometimes. When we think of an accident, we quite often think about it as being no one's fault and something that could not have been avoided. The truth is that most accidents are caused by human error, which means someone has done something they shouldn't have done or, just as importantly, not done something they should have done.

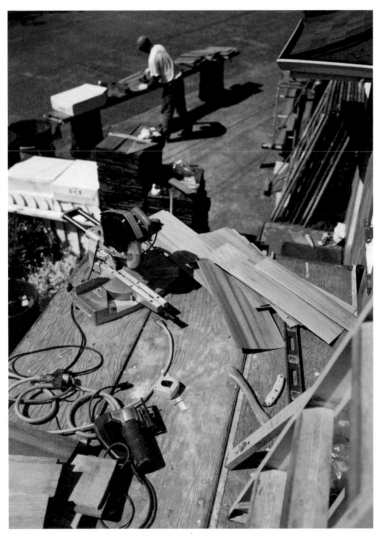
Accidents can happen if your work area is untidy

Accidents often happen when someone is hurrying, not paying enough attention to what they are doing or they have not received the correct training.

If an accident happens, you or the person it happened to may be lucky and will not be injured. More often, an accident will result in an injury which may be minor (e.g. a cut or a bruise) or possibly major (e.g. loss of a limb). Accidents can also be fatal. The most common causes of fatal accidents in the construction industry are:

- falling from scaffolding
- being hit by falling objects and materials
- falling through fragile roofs
- being hit by forklifts or lorries
- electrocution.

Ill health

While working in the construction industry, you will be exposed to substances or situations that may be harmful to your health. Some of these health risks may not be noticeable straight away and it may take years for **symptoms** to be noticed and recognised.

Ill health can result from:

- exposure to dust (such as asbestos), which can cause breathing problems and cancer
- exposure to solvents or chemicals, which can cause **dermatitis** and other skin problems
- lifting heavy or difficult loads, which can cause back injury and pulled muscles
- exposure to loud noise, which can cause hearing problems and deafness
- using vibrating tools, which can cause **vibration white finger** and other problems with the hands.

Everyone has a responsibility for health and safety in the construction industry but accidents and health problems still happen too often. Make sure you do what you can to prevent them.

Definition

Symptom – a sign of illness or disease (e.g. difficulty breathing, a sore hand or a lump under the skin)

Definition

Dermatitis – a skin condition where the affected area is red, itchy and sore

Vibration white finger – a condition that can be caused by using vibrating machinery (usually for very long periods of time). The blood supply to the fingers is reduced which causes pain, tingling and sometimes spasms (shaking)

Staying healthy

As well as keeping an eye out for hazards, you must also make sure that you look after yourself and stay healthy. One of the easiest ways to do this is to wash your hands on a regular basis. By washing your hands you are preventing hazardous substances from entering your body through ingestion (swallowing). You should always wash your hands after going to the toilet and before eating or drinking.

Always wash your hands to prevent ingesting hazardous substances

Definition

Barrier cream – a cream used to protect the skin from damage or infection

Definition

Corrosive – a substance that can damage things it comes into contact with (e.g. material, skin)

Toxic – poisonous

Contamination – when harmful chemicals or substances pollute something (e.g. water)

Other precautions that you can take are ensuring that you wear **barrier cream**, the correct PPE and only drink water that is labelled as drinking water. Remember that some health problems do not show symptoms straight away and what you do now can affect you much later in life.

Welfare facilities

Welfare facilities are things such as toilets, which must be provided by your employer to ensure a safe and healthy workplace. There are several things that your employer must provide to meet welfare standards and these are:

- Toilets – the number of toilets provided depends upon the number of people who are intended to use them. Males and females can use the same toilets providing there is a lock on the inside of the door. Toilets should be flushable with water or, if this is not possible, with chemicals.

- Washing facilities – employers must provide a basin large enough to allow people to wash their hands, face and forearms. Washing facilities must have hot and cold running water as well as soap and a means of drying your hands. Showers may be needed if the work is very dirty or if workers are exposed to **corrosive** and **toxic** substances.

- Drinking water – there should be a supply of clean drinking water available, either from a tap connected to the mains or from bottled water. Taps connected to the mains need to be clearly labelled as drinking water and bottled drinking water must be stored in a separate area to prevent **contamination**.

- Storage or dry room – every building site must have an area where workers can store the clothes that they do not wear on site, such as coats and motorcycle helmets. If this area is to be used as a drying room then adequate heating must also be provided in order to allow clothes to dry.

- Lunch area – every site must have facilities that can be used for taking breaks and lunch well away from the work area. These facilities must provide shelter from the wind and rain and be heated as required. There should be access to tables and chairs, a kettle or urn for boiling water and a means of heating food, such as a microwave.

When working in an occupied house, you should make arrangements with the client to use the facilities in their house.

On the job: Scaffolding safety

Ralph and Vijay are working on the second level of some scaffolding clearing debris. Ralph suggests that, to speed up the task, they should throw the debris over the edge of the scaffolding into a skip below. The building Ralph and Vijay are working on is on a main road and the skip is not in a closed off area. What do you think of Ralph's idea? What are your reasons for this answer?

Manual handling

Manual handling means lifting and moving a piece of equipment or material from one place to another without using machinery. Lifting and moving loads by hand is one of the most common causes of injury at work. Most injuries caused by manual handling result from years of lifting items that are too heavy, are awkward shapes or sizes, or from using the wrong technique. However, it is also possible to cause a lifetime of back pain with just one single lift.

Poor manual handling can cause injuries such as muscle strain, pulled ligaments and hernias. The most common injury by far is spinal injury. Spinal injuries are very serious because there is very little that doctors can do to correct them and, in extreme cases, workers have been left paralysed.

Poor manual handling techniques can lead to serious permanent injury

What you can do to avoid injury

The first and most important thing you can do to avoid injury from lifting is to receive proper manual handling training. Kinetic lifting is a way of lifting objects that reduces the chance of injury and is covered in more detail on the next page.

Before you lift anything you should ask yourself some simple questions:

- Does the object need to be moved?

- Can I use something to help me lift the object? A mechanical aid such as a forklift or crane or a manual aid such as a wheelbarrow may be more appropriate than a person.

- Can I reduce the weight by breaking down the load? Breaking down a load into smaller and more manageable weights may mean that more journeys are needed, but it will also reduce the risk of injury.

- Do I need help? Asking for help to lift a load is not a sign of weakness and team lifting will greatly reduce the risk of injury.

- How much can I lift safely? The recommended maximum weight a person can lift is 25 kg but this is only an average weight and each person is different. The amount that a person can lift will depend on their physique, age and experience.

- Where is the object going? Make sure that any obstacles in your path are out of the way before you lift. You also need to make sure there is somewhere to put the object when you get there.

- Am I trained to lift? The quickest way to receive a manual handling injury is to use the wrong lifting technique.

Lifting correctly (kinetic lifting)

When lifting any load it is important to keep the correct posture and to use the correct technique.

The correct posture before lifting:

- feet shoulder width apart with one foot slightly in front of the other
- knees should be bent
- back must be straight
- arms should be as close to the body as possible
- grip must be firm using the whole hand and not just the finger tips.

The correct technique when lifting:

- approach the load squarely facing the direction of travel
- adopt the correct posture (as above)
- place hands under the load and pull the load close to your body
- lift the load using your legs and not your back.

When lowering a load you must also adopt the correct posture and technique:

- bend at the knees, not the back
- adjust the load to avoid trapping fingers
- release the load.

Remember

Even light loads can cause back problems so, when lifting anything, always take care to avoid twisting or stretching

Think before lifting

Adopt the correct posture before lifting

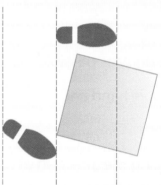

Get a good grip on the load

Adopt the correct posture when lifting

Move smoothly with the load

Adopt the correct posture and technique when lowering

Fire and fire-fighting equipment

Fires can start almost anywhere and at any time but a fire needs three things to burn. These are:

1. fuel

2. heat

3. oxygen.

This can be shown in what is known as 'the triangle of fire'. If any of the sides of the triangle are removed, the fire cannot burn and it will go out.

Find out

What fire risks are there in the construction industry? Think about some of the materials (fuel) and heat sources that could make up two of the sides of 'the triangle of fire'

Figure 2.1 The triangle of fire

Remember:

- Remove the fuel and there is nothing to burn so the fire will go out.

- Remove the heat and the fire will go out.

- Remove the oxygen and the fire will go out as fire needs oxygen to survive.

Fires can be classified according to the type of material that is involved:

- Class A – wood, paper, textiles etc.

- Class B – flammable liquids, petrol, oil etc.

- Class C – flammable gases, liquefied petroleum gas (**LPG**), propane etc.

- Class D – metal, metal powder etc.

- Class E – electrical equipment.

Fire-fighting equipment

There are several types of fire-fighting equipment, such as fire blankets and fire extinguishers. Each type is designed to be the most effective at putting out a particular class of fire and some types should never be used in certain types of fire.

Fire extinguishers

A fire extinguisher is a metal canister containing a substance that can put out a fire. There are several different types and it is important that you learn which type should be used on specific classes of fires. This is because if you use the wrong type, you may make the fire worse or risk severely injuring yourself.

Fire extinguishers are now all one colour (red) but they have a band of colour which shows what substance is inside.

Water

The coloured band is red and this type of extinguisher can be used on Class A fires. Water extinguishers can also be used on Class C fires in order to cool the area down.

A water fire extinguisher should NEVER be used to put out an electrical or burning fat/oil fire. This is because electrical current can carry along the jet of water back to the person holding the extinguisher, electrocuting them. Putting water on to burning fat or oil will make the fire worse as the fire will 'explode', potentially causing serious injury.

Water fire extinguisher

Foam fire extinguisher

Foam

The coloured band is cream and this type of extinguisher can also be used on Class A fires. A foam extinguisher can also be used on a Class B fire if the liquid is not flowing and on a Class C fire if the gas is in liquid form.

Carbon dioxide (CO_2)

The coloured band is black and the extinguisher can be used on Class A, B, C and E fires.

Dry powder

The coloured band is blue and this type of extinguisher can be used on all classes of fire. The powder puts out the fire by knocking down the flames.

Fire blankets

Fire blankets are normally found in kitchens or

Carbon dioxide (CO_2) extinguisher

canteens as they are good at putting out cooking fires. They are made of a fireproof material and work by smothering the fire and stopping any more oxygen from getting to it, thus putting it out. A fire blanket can also be used if a person is on fire.

It is important to remember that when you put out a fire with a fire blanket, you need to take extra care as you will have to get quite close to the fire.

Dry powder extinguisher

A fire blanket

What to do in the event of a fire

During **induction** to any workplace, you will be made aware of the fire procedure as well as where the fire assembly points (also known as **muster points**) are and what the alarm sounds like. On hearing the alarm you must stop what you are doing and make your way to the nearest muster point. This is so that everyone can be accounted for. If you do not go to the muster point or if you leave before someone has taken your name, someone may risk their life to go back into the fire to get you.

When you hear the alarm, you should not stop to gather any belongings and you must not run. If you discover a fire, you must only try to fight the fire if it is blocking your exit or if it is small. Only when you have been given the all-clear can you re-enter the site or building.

Definition

Induction – a formal introduction you will receive when you start any new job, where you will be shown around, shown where the toilets and canteen etc. are, and told what to do if there is a fire

Safety signs

Safety signs can be found in many areas of the workplace and they are put up in order to:

- warn of any **hazards**
- prevent accidents
- inform where things are
- tell you what to do in certain areas.

Definition

Hazard – a danger or risk

Types of safety sign

There are many different safety signs but each will usually fit into one of four categories:

Figure 2.2 A prohibition sign

1. Prohibition signs – these tell you that something MUST NOT be done. They always have a white background and a red circle with a red line through it.

Figure 2.3 A mandatory sign

2. Mandatory signs – these tell you that something MUST be done. They are also circular but have a white symbol on a blue background.

Figure 2.4 A warning sign

3. Warning signs – these signs are there to alert you to a specific hazard. They are triangular and have a yellow background and a black border.

Figure 2.5 An information sign

4. Information signs – these give you useful information like the location of things (e.g. a first aid point). They can be square or rectangular and are green with a white symbol.

Figure 2.6 A safety sign with both symbol and words

Most signs only have symbols that let you know what they are saying. Others have some words as well, for example, a no smoking sign might have a cigarette in a red circle, with a red line crossing through the cigarette and the words 'No smoking' underneath.

Personal protective equipment (PPE)

Personal protective equipment (PPE) is a form of defence against accidents or injury and comes in the form of articles of clothing. This is not to say that PPE is the only way of preventing accidents or injury. It should be used together with all the other methods of staying healthy and safe in the workplace (i.e. equipment, training, regulations and laws etc.).

PPE must be supplied by your employer free of charge and you have responsibility as an employee to look after it and use it whenever it is required.

Types of PPE

There are certain parts of the body that require protection from hazards during work and each piece of PPE must be suitable for the job and used properly.

Head protection

There are several different types of head protection but the one most commonly used in construction is the safety helmet (or hard hat). This is used to protect the head from falling objects and knocks and has an adjustable strap to ensure a snug fit. Some safety helmets come with attachments for ear defenders or eye protection. Safety helmets are meant to be worn directly on the head and must not be worn over any other type of hat.

Remember

Make sure you take notice of safety signs in the workplace – they have been put up for a reason!

Remember

PPE only works properly if it is being used and used correctly!

A safety helmet

Eye protection

Eye protection is used to protect the eyes from dust and flying debris. The three main types are:

1. Safety goggles – made of a durable plastic and used when there is a danger of dust getting into the eyes or a chance of impact injury.

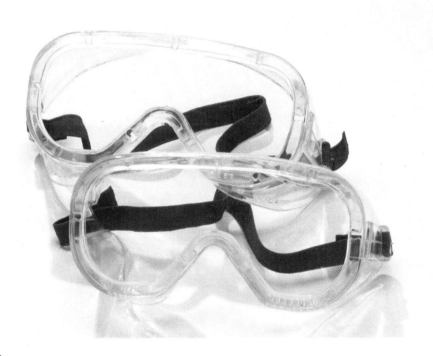

Safety goggles

2. Safety spectacles – these are also made from a durable plastic but give less protection than goggles. This is because they don't fully enclose the eyes and so only protect from flying debris.

Safety spectacles

3. Facemasks – again made of durable plastic, facemasks protect the entire face from flying debris. They do not, however, protect the eyes from dust.

Foot protection

Safety boots or shoes are used to protect the feet from falling objects and to prevent sharp objects such as nails from injuring the foot. Safety boots should have a steel toe-cap and steel mid-sole.

Safety boots

Hearing protection

Hearing protection is used to prevent damage to the ears caused by very loud noise. There are several types of hearing protection available but the two most common types are earplugs and ear defenders.

Ear-plugs

1. Ear-plugs – these are small fibre plugs that are inserted into the ear and used when the noise is not too severe. When using ear-plugs, make sure that you have clean hands before inserting them and never use plugs that have been used by somebody else.

Ear defenders

2. Ear defenders – these are worn to cover the entire ear and are connected to a band that fits over the top of the head. They are used when there is excessive noise and must be cleaned regularly.

Respiratory protection

Respiratory protection is used to prevent the worker from breathing in any dust or fumes that may be hazardous. The main type of respiratory protection is the dust mask.

Dust masks are used when working in a dusty environment and are lightweight, comfortable and easy to fit. They should be worn by only one person and must be disposed of at the end of the working day. Dust masks will only offer protection from non-toxic dust so, if the worker is to be exposed to toxic dust or fumes, a full respiratory system should be used.

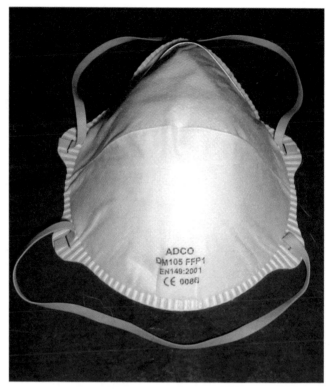

A dust mask

Hand protection

There are several types of hand protection and each type must be used for the correct task. For example, wearing lightweight rubber gloves to move glass will not offer much protection so leather gauntlets must be used. Plastic-coated gloves will protect you from certain chemicals and Kevlar® gloves offer cut resistance. To make sure you are wearing the most suitable type of glove for the task, you need to look first at what is going to be done and then match the type of glove to that task.

Safety gloves

Reporting accidents

When an accident occurs, there are certain things that must be done. All accidents need to be reported and recorded in the accident book and the injured person must report to a trained first aider in order to receive treatment. Serious accidents must be reported under the Reporting of Injuries, Diseases and Dangerous Occurrences Regulations 1995 (RIDDOR). Under RIDDOR your employer must report to the HSE any accident that results in:

- death

- major injury

- an injury that means the injured person is not at work for more than three consecutive days.

The accident book

The accident book is completed by the person who had the accident or, if this is not possible, someone who is representing the injured person.

The accident book will ask for some basic details about the accident, including:

- who was involved

- what happened

- where it happened

- the day and time of the accident

- any witnesses to the accident

- the address of the injured person

- what PPE was being worn

- what first aid treatment was given.

Figure 2.7 A typical accident book page

Report of an Accident, Dangerous Occurrence or Near Miss

Date of incident _____   **Time of incident** _____

Location of incident _____

Details of person involved in accident

Name _____   Date of birth _____   Sex _____

Address _____

_____

_____ Occupation _____

Date off work (if applicable) _____   **Date returning to work** _____

Nature of injury _____

Management of injury   ☐ First Aid only   ☐ Advised to see doctor

                           ☐ Sent to casualty   ☐ Admitted to hospital

Account of accident, dangerous occurrence or near miss
(Continued on separate sheet if necessary)

[ ]

Witnesses to the incident
(Names, addresses and occupations)

[ ]

Was the injured person wearing PPE? If yes, what PPE? _____

_____

Signature of person completing form _____

Occupation _____   **Date** _____

Definition

Proactive – taking action *before* something happens (e.g. an accident)

Reactive – taking action *after* something happens

As well as reporting accidents, 'near misses' must also be reported. This is because near misses are often the accidents of the future. Reporting near misses might identify a problem and can prevent accidents from happening in the future. This allows a company to be **proactive** rather than **reactive**.

Risk assessments

A risk assessment is where the dangers of an activity are measured against the likelihood of accidents taking place. People carry out risk assessments hundreds of times each day without even knowing it. For example, every time we cross the road we do a risk assessment without even thinking about it.

In the construction industry, risk assessments are done by experienced people who are able to identify what risks each task has. They are then able to put measures in place to control the risks they have identified. At some point in your career, you will have to carry out a risk assessment. You will be given proper training in how to do this but, until then, it is still important that you understand how risk assessments work. Below is an example of an everyday situation (crossing the road) and how a risk assessment would be carried out for this.

Step 1

Identify the hazards (the dangers) – in this situation the hazards are vehicles travelling at speed.

Step 2

Identify who will be at risk – the person crossing the road will be at risk, as will any drivers on the road who might have to swerve to avoid that person.

Step 3

Calculate the risk from the hazard against the likelihood of an accident taking place – the risk from the hazard is quite high because if an accident were to happen, the injury could be very serious. However, the likelihood of an accident happening is low because the chances of the person being hit while crossing are minimal.

Step 4

Introduce measures to reduce risk – in this case crossing the road at traffic lights or pedestrian crossings reduces risk.

Step 5

Monitor the risk – changes might need to be made to the risk assessment if there are any changes to the risks involved. In our example, changes might be traffic lights being out of order or an increase in the speed limit on the road.

On the job: Unidentified material

Craig and Kevin are clearing out a basement of all fixtures and fittings in preparation for a job. They uncover some white plaster-like material covering a heating pipe. They have never seen this type of material before and are not sure what it could be. Craig suggests that they just remove it so that they can get the job done. Kevin is not sure if this is such a good idea and wants to tell their boss about the material before they remove it. Who do you think has given the best suggestion? Why?

Knowledge check

1. Name five pieces of health and safety legislation that affect the construction industry.

2. What does HSE stand for? What does it do?

3. What does COSHH stand for?

4. What does RIDDOR stand for?

5. What might happen to you or your employer if a health and safety law is broken?

6. What are the two most common risks to construction workers?

7. State two things that you can do to avoid injury when lifting loads using manual handling techniques.

8. What three elements cause a fire and keep it burning?

9. What class(es) of fire can be put out with a carbon dioxide (CO_2) extinguisher?

10. What does a prohibition sign mean?

11. Describe how you would identify a warning sign.

12. Name the six different types of PPE.

13. Who fills in an accident report form?

14. Why is it important to report 'near misses'?

15. Briefly explain what a risk assessment is.

chapter 3

Working at height

OVERVIEW

Most construction trades require frequent use of some type of working platform or access equipment. Working off the ground can be dangerous and the greater the height the more serious the risk of injury. This chapter will give you a summary of some of the most common types of access equipment and provide information on how they should be used, maintained and checked to ensure that the risks to you and others are minimal.

This chapter will cover the following:

- General safety considerations
- Stepladders and ladders
- Roof work
- Trestle platforms
- Hop-ups
- Scaffolding.

General safety considerations

You will need to be able to identify potential hazards associated with working at height, as well as hazards associated with equipment. It is essential that access equipment is well maintained and checked regularly for any deterioration or faults, which could compromise the safety of someone using the equipment and anyone else in the work area. Although obviously not as important as people, equipment can also be damaged by the use of faulty access equipment. When maintenance checks are carried out they should be properly recorded. This provides very important information that helps to prevent accidents.

Risk assessment

Before any work is carried out at height, a thorough risk assessment needs to be completed. Your supervisor or someone else more experienced will do this while you are still training, but it is important that you understand what is involved so that you are able to carry out an assessment in the future.

For a working at height risk assessment to be valid and effective a number of questions must be answered:

1. How is access and **egress** to the work area to be achieved?

2. What type of work is to be carried out?

3. How long is the work likely to last?

4. How many people will be carrying out the task?

5. How often will this work be carried out?

6. What is the condition of the existing structure (if any) and the surroundings?

7. Is adverse weather likely to affect the work and workers?

8. How competent are the workforce and their supervisors?

9. Is there a risk to the public and work colleagues?

Definition

Egress - an exit or way out

Duties

Your employer has a duty to provide and maintain safe plant and equipment, which includes scaffold access equipment and systems of work.

You have a duty:

- to comply with safety rules and procedures relating to access equipment

- to take positive steps to understand the hazards in the workplace and report things you consider likely to lead to danger, for example a missing handrail on a working platform

- not to tamper with or modify equipment.

Stepladders and ladders

Stepladders

A stepladder has a prop, which when folded out allows the ladder to be used without having to lean it against something. Stepladders are one of the most frequently used pieces of access equipment in the construction industry and are often used every day. This means that they are not always treated with the respect they demand. Stepladders are often misused – they should only be used for work that will take a few minutes to complete. When work is likely to take longer than this, a sturdier alternative should be found.

When stepladders are used, the following safety points should be observed:

- Ensure the ground on which the stepladder is to be placed is firm and level. If the ladder rocks or sinks into the ground it should not be used for the work.

- Always open the steps fully.

- Never work off the top tread of the stepladder.

- Always keep your knees below the top tread.

- Never use stepladders to gain additional height on another working platform.

Did you know?

Only a fully trained and competent person is allowed to erect any kind of working platform or access equipment. You should therefore not attempt to erect this type of equipment unless this describes you!

- Always look for the kitemark, which shows that the ladder has been made to British Standards.

Figure 3.1 British Standards Institution Kitemark

A number of other safety points need to be observed depending on the type of stepladder being used.

Wooden stepladder

Before using a wooden stepladder:

- Check for loose screws, nuts, bolts and hinges.
- Check that the tie ropes between the two sets of **stiles** are in good condition and not frayed.
- Check for splits or cracks in the stiles.
- Check that the treads are not loose or split.

Never paint any part of a wooden stepladder as this can hide defects, which may cause the ladder to fail during use, causing injury.

Definition

Stiles – the side pieces of a stepladder into which the steps are set

Wooden stepladder

Aluminium stepladder

Before using an aluminium
stepladder:

- Check for damage to stiles
  and treads to see whether
  they are twisted, badly
  dented or loose.

- Avoid working close to
  live electricity supplies as
  aluminium will conduct
  electricity.

Aluminium stepladder

Fibreglass stepladder

Before using a fibreglass stepladder, check for damage to stiles and treads.
Once damaged, fibreglass stepladders cannot be repaired and must be
disposed of.

Ladders

A ladder, unlike a stepladder, does not have a prop and so has to be leant
against something in order for it to be used. Together with stepladders,
ladders are one of the most common pieces of equipment used to carry out
work at heights and gain access to the work area.

As with stepladders, ladders are also available in timber, aluminium and
fibreglass and require similar checks before use.

Safety tip

If any faults are revealed
when checking a wooden
stepladder, it should be
taken out of use, reported
to the person in charge
and a warning notice
attached to it to stop
anyone using it

Find out

What are the advantages
and disadvantages of
each type of stepladder?

**Did you
know?**

Stepladders should be
stored under cover to
protect from damage
such as rust or rotting

Safety tip

Ladders must NEVER be
repaired once damaged
and must be disposed of

Pole ladder

Ladder types

Pole ladder

These are single ladders and are available in a range of lengths. They are most commonly used for access to scaffolding platforms. Pole ladders are made from timber and must be stored under cover and flat, supported evenly along their length to prevent them sagging and twisting. They should be checked for damage or defects every time before being used.

Extension ladder

Extension ladders have two or more interlocking lengths, which can be slid together for convenient storage or slid apart to the desired length when in use.

Extension ladders are available in timber, aluminium and fibreglass. Aluminium types are the most favoured as they are lightweight yet strong and available in double and triple extension types. Although also very strong, fibreglass versions are heavy, making them difficult to manoeuvre.

Aluminium extension ladder

Erecting and using a ladder

The following points should be noted when considering the use of a ladder:

- As with stepladders, ladders are not designed for work of long duration. Alternative working platforms should be considered if the work will take longer than a few minutes.

- The work should not require the use of both hands. One hand should be free to hold the ladder.

- You should be able to do the work without stretching.

- You should make sure that the ladder can be adequately secured to prevent it slipping on the surface it is leaning against.

Pre-use checks

Before using a ladder check its general condition. Make sure that:

- no rungs are damaged or missing

- the stiles are not damaged

- no **tie-rods** are missing

- no repairs have been made to the ladder.

In addition, for wooden ladders ensure that:

- they have not been painted, which may hide defects or damage

- there is no decay or rot

- the ladder is not twisted or warped.

Erecting a ladder

Observe the following guidelines when erecting a ladder:

- Ensure you have a solid, level base.

- Do not pack anything under either (or both) of the stiles to level it.

Did you know?

On average in the UK, 14 people a year die at work falling from ladders; nearly 1200 suffer major injuries (source: Health and Safety Executive)

Definition

Tie-rods – metal rods underneath the rungs of a ladder that give extra support to the rungs

Remember

You must carry out a thorough risk assessment before working from a ladder. Ask yourself, 'Would I be safer using an alternative method?'

- If the ladder is too heavy to put it in position on your own, get someone to help.

- Ensure that there is at least a four-rung overlap on each extension section.

- Never rest the ladder on plastic guttering as it may break, causing the ladder to slip and the user to fall.

- Where the base of the ladder is in an exposed position, ensure it is adequately guarded so that no one knocks it or walks in to it.

- The ladder should be secured at both the top and bottom. The bottom of the ladder can be secured by a second person, however this person must not leave the base of the ladder whilst it is in use.

- The angle of the ladder should be a ratio of 1:4 (or 75°). This means that the bottom of ladder is 1 m away from the wall for every 4 m in height (see Figure 3.2).

- The top of the ladder must extend at least 1 m, or 5 rungs, above its landing point.

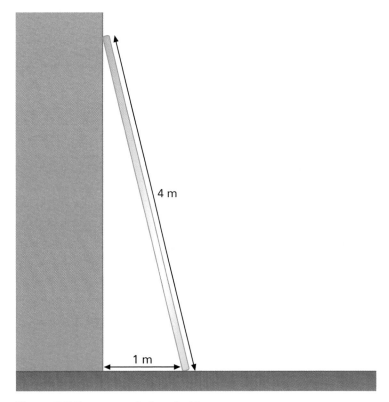

4 m

1 m

Figure 3.2 Correct angle for a ladder

Roof work

When carrying out any work on a roof, a roof ladder or **crawling board** must be used. Roof work also requires the use of edge protection or, where this is not possible, a safety harness.

Definition

Crawling board – a board or platform placed on roof joists which spread the weight of the worker allowing the work to be carried out safely

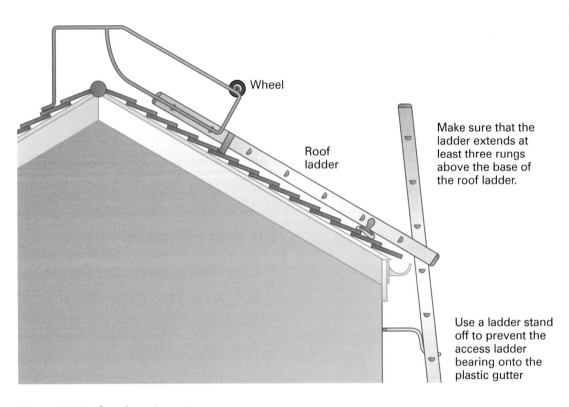

Wheel

Roof ladder

Make sure that the ladder extends at least three rungs above the base of the roof ladder.

Use a ladder stand off to prevent the access ladder bearing onto the plastic gutter

Figure 3.3 Roof work equipment

The roof ladder is rolled up the surface of the roof and over the ridge tiles, just enough to allow the ladder to be turned over and the ladder hook allowed to bear on the tiles on the other side of the roof. This hook prevents the roof ladder sliding down the roof once it is accessed.

Trestle platforms

A trestle is a frame upon which a platform or other type of surface (e.g. a table top) can be placed. A trestle should be used rather than a ladder for work that will take longer than a few minutes to complete. Trestle platforms are composed of the frame and the platform (sometimes called a stage).

Frames

A-frames

These are most commonly used by carpenters and painters. As the name suggests, the frame is in the shape of a capital A and can be made from timber, aluminium or fibreglass. Two are used together to support a platform (a scaffold or staging board). See Figure 3.4.

Safety tip

A-frame trestles should never be used as stepladders as they are not designed for this purpose

When using A-frames:

- they should always be opened fully and, in the same way as stepladders, must be placed on firm, level ground

- the platform width should be no less than 450 mm

- the overhang of the board at each end of the platform should be not more than four times its thickness.

Figure 3.4 A-frame trestles with scaffold board

Steel trestles

These are sturdier than A-frame trestles and are adjustable in height. They are also capable of providing a wider platform than timber trestles – see Figure 3.5. As with the A-frame type, they must be used only on firm and level ground but the trestle itself should be placed on a flat scaffold board on top of the ground. Trestles should not be placed more than 1.2 m apart.

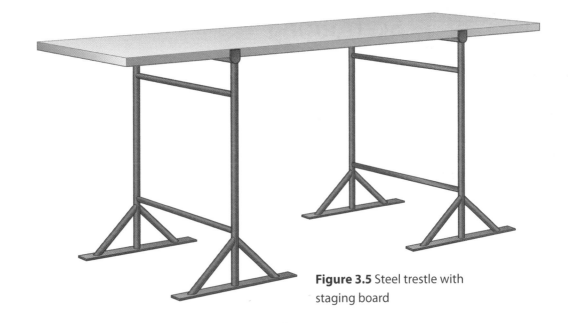

Figure 3.5 Steel trestle with staging board

Platforms

Scaffold boards

To ensure that scaffold boards provide a safe working platform, before using them check that they:

- are not split
- are not twisted or warped
- have no large knots, which cause weakness.

Staging boards

These are designed to span a greater distance than scaffold boards and can offer a 600 mm wide working platform. They are ideal for use with trestles.

Hop-ups

Also known as step-ups, these are ideal for reaching low-level work that can be carried out in a relatively short period of time. A hop-up needs to be of sturdy construction and have a base of not less than 600 mm by 500 mm. Hop-ups have the disadvantage that they are heavy and awkward to move around.

Scaffolding

Tubular scaffold is the most commonly used type of scaffolding within the construction industry. There are two types of tubular scaffold:

1. Independent scaffold – free-standing scaffold that does not rely on any part of the building to support it (although it must be tied to the building to provide additional stability).

2. Putlog scaffold – scaffolding that is attached to the building via the entry of some of the poles into holes left in the brickwork by the bricklayer. The poles stay in position until the construction is complete and give the scaffold extra support.

No one other than a qualified **carded scaffolder** is allowed to erect or alter scaffolding. Although you are not allowed to erect or alter this type of scaffold, you must be sure it is safe before you work on it. You should ask yourself a number of questions to assess the condition and suitability of the scaffold before you use it:

- Are there any signs attached to the scaffold which state that it is incomplete or unsafe?

- Is the scaffold overloaded with materials such as bricks?

- Are the platforms cluttered with waste materials?

- Are there adequate guardrails and scaffold boards in place?

- Does the scaffold actually *look* safe?

- Is there the correct access to and from the scaffold?

- Are the various scaffold components in the correct place (see Figure 3.6)?

- Have the correct types of fittings been used (see Figure 3.7)?

Remember

If you have any doubts about the safety of scaffolding, report them. You could very well prevent serious injury or even someone's death

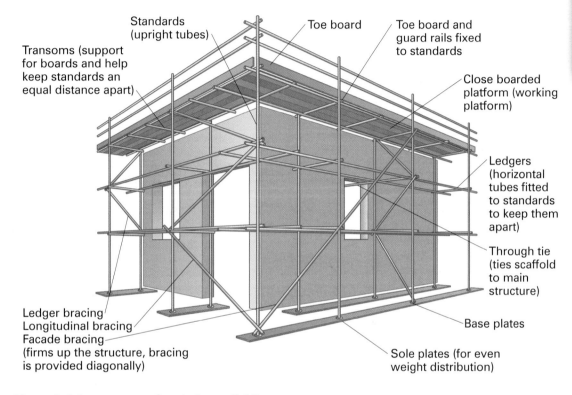

Figure 3.6 Components of a tubular scaffolding structure

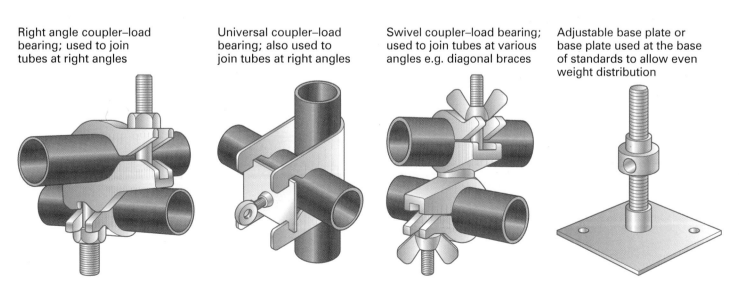

Right angle coupler–load bearing; used to join tubes at right angles

Universal coupler–load bearing; also used to join tubes at right angles

Swivel coupler–load bearing; used to join tubes at various angles e.g. diagonal braces

Adjustable base plate or base plate used at the base of standards to allow even weight distribution

Figure 3.7 Types of scaffold fittings

Mobile tower scaffolds

Mobile tower scaffolds are so called because they can be moved around without being dismantled. Lockable wheels make this possible and they are used extensively throughout the construction industry by many different trades. A tower can be made from either traditional steel tubes and fittings or aluminium, which is lightweight and easy to move. The aluminium type of tower is normally specially designed and is referred to as a 'proprietary tower'.

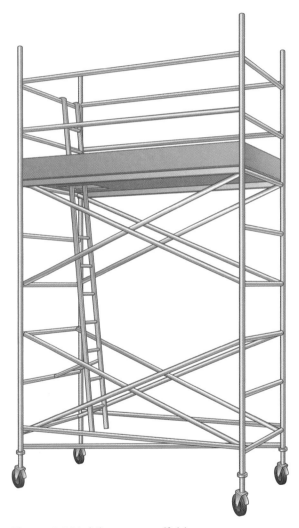

Figure 3.8 Mobile tower scaffold

Low towers

These are a smaller version of the standard mobile tower scaffold and are designed specifically for use by one person. They have a recommended working height of no more than 2.5 m and a safe working load of 150 kg. They are lightweight and easily transported and stored.

Figure 3.9 Low tower scaffold

These towers require no assembly other than the locking into place of the platform and handrails. However, you still require training before you use one and you must ensure that the manufacturer's instructions are followed when setting up and working from this type of platform.

Erecting a tower scaffold

It is essential that tower scaffolds are situated on a firm and level base. The stability of any tower depends on the height in relation the size of the base:

- For use inside a building, the height should be no more than three-and-a-half times the smallest base length.

- For outside use, the height should be no more than three times the smallest base length.

The height of a tower can be increased providing the area of the base is increased **proportionately**. The base area can be increased by fitting outriggers to each corner of the tower.

For mobile towers, the wheels must be in the locked position whilst they are in use and unlocked only when they are being re-positioned.

There are several important points you should observe when working from a scaffold tower:

- Any working platform above 2 m high must be fitted with guardrails and toe boards. Guard rails may also be required at heights of less than 2 m if there is a risk of falling on to potential hazards below, i.e. reinforcing rods. Guardrails must be fitted at a minimum height of 950 mm.

- If guardrails and toe boards are needed, they must be positioned on all four sides of the platform.

- Any tower higher than 9 m must be secured to the structure.

- Towers must not exceed 12 m in height unless they have been specifically designed for that purpose.

- The working platform of any tower must be fully boarded and be at least 600 mm wide.

- If the working platform is to be used for materials then the minimum width must be 800 mm.

- All towers must have their own access and this should be by an internal ladder.

Definition

Proportionately – in proportion to the size of something else

Safety tip

Mobile towers must *only* be moved when they are free of people, tools and materials

Safety tip

Never climb a scaffold tower on the outside as this can cause it to tip over

FAQ

When using a ladder, is it OK to stand on the very top rung in order to reach something if I am quick? I'm only going to be a second.

You are putting yourself at risk if you do stand on the top rung and you would also be breaking health and safety law. It doesn't matter how quick you are, don't risk it and use a longer ladder or some scaffolding.

I haven't got enough trestles to support a scaffold board but it looks safe enough – is this OK?

If the scaffold board is not well supported by having trestles no further than 1.2 m apart, it could collapse or break. Make sure you have enough trestles.

On the job: Ryan's tower

Ryan is putting together a tower scaffold. He realises that he does not have enough diagonal supports for the tower so he decides to leave every other support out. Ryan is sure that this will be OK as the tower will still have some diagonal support. What do you think of Ryan's idea?

Knowledge check

1. Name four different methods of gaining height while working.

2. What must be done before any work at height is carried out?

3. What are your three health and safety duties when working at height?

4. As a rule, what is the maximum time you should work from a ladder or stepladder?

5. How should a wooden stepladder be checked before use?

6. When storing a wooden pole ladder, why does it need to be evenly supported along its length?

7. Explain the 1:4 (or 75°) ratio rule which should be observed when erecting a ladder.

8. When should a trestle platform be used?

9. What two types of board can be used as a platform with a trestle frame?

10. Why should you only use a specially designed hop-up?

11. There are two types of tubular scaffolding – what are they and how do they differ?

12. What are the eight questions you should ask yourself before using scaffolding?

13. In order to increase the height of a tower scaffold, what else has to be increased and by how much?

14. How high should scaffold guardrails be?

15. What is the only way you should access scaffolding?

Tools and equipment

chapter **4**

OVERVIEW

This chapter provides a basic introduction to some of the tools and equipment used within the painting and decorating profession. The tools and equipment described are those most commonly used for both preparation and a variety of application methods. We will also look at some of the basic maintenance tasks required to ensure that the tools are kept in good condition. The equipment that you build up throughout your working life helps you make a living. You should therefore look after your tools, which will also help avoid any unnecessary and costly repairs and replacements.

In this chapter you will learn about:

- Preparation tools and equipment

- Painting tools and equipment

- Paper hanging tools and equipment

- Specialist tools and equipment

- Glazing tools and equipment.

Preparation tools and equipment

Before you start any painting or decorating task, you will need to prepare the area and surfaces you are going to work on. If you don't do this, the results will be poor and you may have to start again, which will cost time and money.

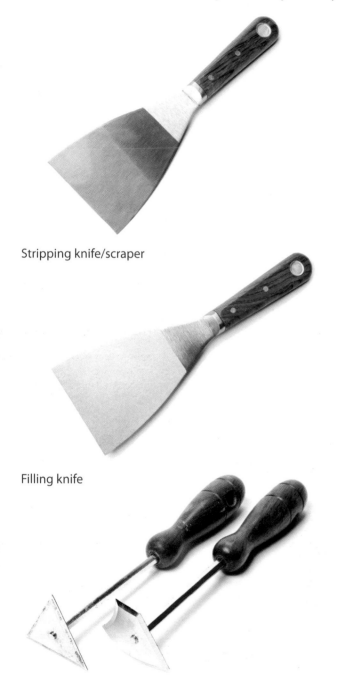

Stripping knife/scraper

Filling knife

Shave hooks (triangular and combination)

Knives and scrapers

Stripping knife/scraper

A stripping knife (or scraper) is used to remove old or flaking paint, wallpaper and other loose debris from surfaces to be decorated. When not in use, it is advisable to clean off the knife and protect the tip with a suitable cover.

Filling knife

A filling knife looks very similar to a stripping knife but is used to apply fillers as part of the preparation process. The blade is made of a thinner gauge metal, which makes it more flexible allowing manipulation of the filler. A filling knife requires the same cleaning and protection as a scraping knife.

Shave hooks

Shave hooks are used to scrape off loose deposits and old coatings from beadings and mouldings during burning off or basic paint removal processes. They can also be used to prepare areas which are to receive fillers. Shave hooks are available in three different shapes: triangular, pear-shaped and a combination of the two. The blade edges should be kept sharp to ensure maximum performance and avoid unnecessary damage to surfaces.

Torches and strippers

LPG torch/gun

LPG (liquefied petroleum gas) torches or guns are used to remove old paint and varnish. They do this by producing a naked flame that makes the area being treated hot, allowing the paint or varnish to be scraped off with a stripping knife or shave hook.

As an alternative to an LPG torch that runs from a large gas canister (see photo), a smaller disposable cartridge type gas torch is also available. These are light and easy to use, although they do produce less heat and have a shorter burning time.

LPG torch/gun

There are a number of safety precautions that should be followed when using this type of equipment and these are dealt with in Chapter 7 Preparation of surfaces (see page 135).

Hot air gun/stripper

Hot air guns or strippers are used in the same way as LPG torches, but they produce hot air via an electrical element rather than a naked flame. This reduces the risk of fire and scorching of surfaces such as timber. In addition, hot air guns/strippers are more suited to use on surfaces where there is a risk of **combustion** or where there is glass present, which could crack due to the high temperature.

Hot air gun/stripper

Remember

LPG torches or guns should never be used to remove lead-based coatings. This is because toxic fumes or dust can be released, which can cause lasting damage to the airways and lungs and possibly permanent breathing problems

Safety tip

Always follow manufacturer's instructions regarding the correct use and maintenance of LPG torches

Definition

Combustion – burning or catching on fire

Steam stripper

Using a steam stripper is a very efficient way of removing surface coverings from both walls and ceilings. However, care must be taken when using this method because over-application of the steam process can result in damage to the covered surface, leading to blistering and/or removal of small areas of plaster finishes. Care must also be taken when using these items on ceilings because the user can be at risk from burns or scalding due to the hot water/steam produced by the stripper.

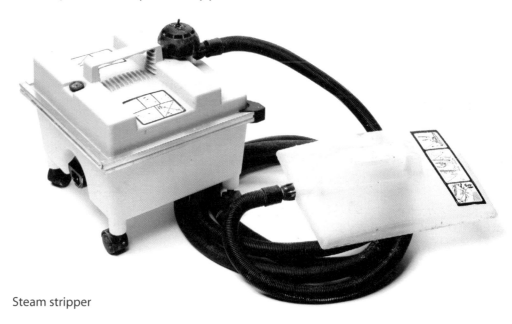

Steam stripper

Brushes

All brushes need to be cleaned thoroughly after use. Leaving traces of material on the bristles could damage them, making the brush useless. Care of brushes depends upon the material from which they are made. It is therefore best to read any manufacturer's instructions on cleaning and storage.

Dusting brush

Dusting brushes are used to remove loose dust, grit and other fine debris from surfaces before applying paint.

Dusting brush

Dustpan and brush

A dustpan and brush can be used for general cleaning before and after decorating and is an important part of the decorator's tool kit. If you fail to remove dust and debris from your work area, it may result in the contamination of surfaces and paint systems, leading to poor workmanship and a damaged reputation.

Dustpan and brush

Wire brush

A wire brush is used to remove loose rust and corrosion from various types of metalwork. They are available with either steel wire or bronze wire bristles. Bronze wire versions are suited to situations where there is a fire hazard as they will not cause sparks.

Wire brush

Rotary wire brush

Rotary wire brushes are used in the same way as ordinary wire brushes, although they are more powerful and less manually demanding to use (i.e. they do some of the work for you).

Rotary wire brush

Abrading equipment

Abrading is an important part of preparing a surface to be decorated. You will often need to remove substances from the surface you are going to work on and abrading can also be useful after decorating, for example if paintwork has dried too quickly and wrinkled.

Abrasive paper

Sometimes known as sandpaper, abrasive paper is grit on flexible backing sheets used to wear down a surface. Abrasive paper is available with different sizes of grit, each suited to a different type of task (e.g. for coarse or fine abrasion). Wet abrasive paper can be used with water to give a very fine abrasion or, when used with mineral oil, for smoothing and polishing metals.

You should always use the correct type of abrasive paper for the job and you should never use hand abrasive paper in a power tool such as an orbital or belt sander. Abrasive papers should be stored in a cool dry place and replaced regularly.

Rubbing blocks

Rubbing blocks are used to support both wet and dry abrasive papers and make handling and working with abrasive papers easier. They are available in wood, plastic, cork or rubber versions.

Rubbing block

Sanders

There are two main types of sander used for the purpose of abrading:

1. orbital sander

2. belt sander.

The orbital sander is the slower of the two, but is lighter and easier to use. It can be used to prepare surfaces ready for painting, including timber, plastic, most metals and previously painted surfaces. This type of sander is more suited to small areas. The belt sander is much faster than the orbital sander and is more suited to larger surface areas.

Safety tip

When using electrical equipment, always follow the manufacturer's instructions for use and check the equipment before you use it to ensure there are no faults, either with the equipment or its power supply lead

Orbital sander

Belt sander

Chapter 7 Preparation of surfaces provides further information on the use of abrading materials (see page 135).

Other types of preparation tools and equipment

Needle gun

Needle guns are used to remove rust from around corroded nuts, bolts, rivets and welds. They can also be used in the preparation of stonework. There are various types of needles available for use with the gun depending on the surface to be prepared. Needle guns are powered by compressed air and great care must be taken to ensure safe operation.

Needle gun

Caulking tool

Caulking tool

Made up of a flexible flat metal blade set in a wooden or plastic handle, a caulking tool is used for applying filler and jointing materials. It is also sometimes used to smooth out decorative coverings applied to plasterboard surfaces. A caulking tool should be maintained in the same way as a filling knife.

Screwdrivers

Screwdrivers

A selection of screwdrivers for removing fixtures and fittings such as switches, sockets and radiators should be kept in your toolkit.

Painting tools and equipment

Find out

What are the pros and cons (advantages/disadvantages) of the different fillings available?

Paint is used to give protection and colour to walls, ceilings and other surfaces. Made up of pigment (the colour) and an oil- or water-based binder, paint can be applied very easily and quickly to give a basic addition of colour or, with the aid of special tools and techniques, paint can also give very creative and striking effects and finishes. For more information on paint application techniques, see Chapter 9 Applying paint and creating special effects (page 191) and Chapter 10 Applying surface coatings (page 221).

Paintbrushes

A brush's bristles, also known as the **filling**, can be either pure bristle (animal hair), man-made fibres, natural fibres or a combination of these. The filling is attached to the handle of the brush via the stock and secured with the use of an adhesive.

After use, a brush must be thoroughly cleaned. This means that all traces of paint should be removed with a suitable solvent. The solvent should then be washed out of the filling with warm soapy water. Brushes should be hung up to dry and should never be put away while still wet or damp.

Always store brushes flat and *never* stand the brush upright on the filling because this will permanently change the shape of the filling and leave the brush useless. Always read the paint manufacturer's instructions regarding their recommended cleaning process.

Flat brush

A flat brush is the type of brush used for the majority of paint and varnish work and is available in a wide variety of sizes and filling types. The 25 mm flat brush is also known as a sash brush as it is normally used for painting sashes and frames. Larger flat brushes, including the 100 mm size, are used mainly for painting walls and ceilings. The handle is usually made from beech or birch, although cheaper varieties with plastic handles are available.

Flat brushes

Radiator brush

A radiator brush is used to apply paint behind radiators and pipes. It has a long flexible handle and is ideal for painting awkward and hard-to-reach areas.

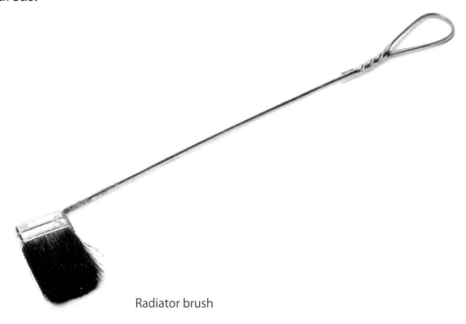

Radiator brush

Crevice brush

Crevice brushes are much the same as radiator brushes but are angled to allow access to the most awkward of areas.

Crevice brush

Lining brush

Lining brushes are used together with a straight edge to produce straight lines. This type of brush is very flat and thin.

Lining brush

Stencil brush

A stencil brush is a short, stumpy brush used for painting on to stencils or around templates.

Stencil brush

Masonry brush

Masonry brushes are used to apply paint to surfaces such as stonework, brick, concrete and **rendering**. They are cheap to buy and very **durable**.

Definition

Rendering – stone or brickwork coated with plaster

Durable – long-lasting

Masonry brush

Fitch

Fitch

A **fitch** is ideal for painting areas difficult to reach with a standard paintbrush and also for more detailed work. They are available in either a flat or round style.

Rollers

A roller can quickly and effectively coat large flat surface areas with paint. Specially shaped rollers are also available for painting corners and other unusually shaped surfaces, although sometimes it can be easier to simply use a brush.

Roller sleeves

The part of the roller that holds the paint is the roller sleeve and it is a plastic tube covered with fabric. The type of sleeve, and thus the type of fabric, chosen depends upon the kind of coating to be applied and the structure of the surface. The sleeve slides onto the frame of the roller. The frame will be either a cage type or a stick type.

Rollers are available in many sizes and can have single or double arms. A double arm roller is available for roller sleeves of 300 mm and above.

Roller frame (single arm cage type)

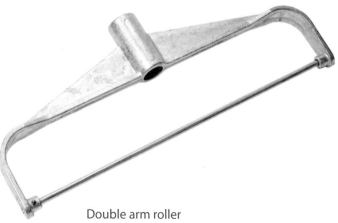

Double arm roller

All rollers must be cleaned thoroughly after use. Always hang them up to dry because if left resting wet on a surface, damage will be caused to the fabric which will seriously affect the finish of future paint applications.

Radiator roller

Radiator rollers are also known as mini rollers and are available in sizes of up to 150 mm. As the name suggests, they are ideal for use on radiators and other small surface areas where the use of a standard roller would be impractical.

Find out

What are the differences between the two types of roller frame (cage and stick)?

Find out

What types of roller fabric are available? What type of decorative or textured effects does each type produce?

Radiator roller

Specialised rollers

There are a number of types of roller designed for specific tasks such as painting pipe work or producing decorative and textured effects. One such roller is the Duet® roller, which is made from uneven pieces of chamois leather attached to a spindle.

Duet® roller

Other types of painting tools and equipment

Paint stirrer

Quite simply, this is used to stir paint, as well as other decorating materials such as varnish and paste. Available in various lengths, they consist of a blade with a series of holes, through which the paint passes as it is stirred. Stirring in this way enables the paint or other liquid to be mixed more thoroughly than if mixed with a stirrer without holes (i.e. with a stick).

Paint stirrer

Paint kettle (work pot)

Paint kettle (work pot)

Made from either plastic or metal, a paint kettle (often known as a work pot) is a convenient way of holding manageable amounts of paint while working from stepladders or other platforms. Always ensure that your paint kettle is thoroughly cleaned out after use in order to avoid contamination of paints and to prolong the life of the kettle.

Brush keep

Brush keep

A brush keep is used to store brushes in a wet state. It works by way of a solvent being placed in a bottle with an evaporating wick. The fumes from the evaporating solvent replace the air in the brush keep, preventing the brushes from drying out.

Extension pole

Extension poles are attached to roller handles in order to give additional reach, thus reducing the need for working on stepladders when painting areas such as ceilings or high walls.

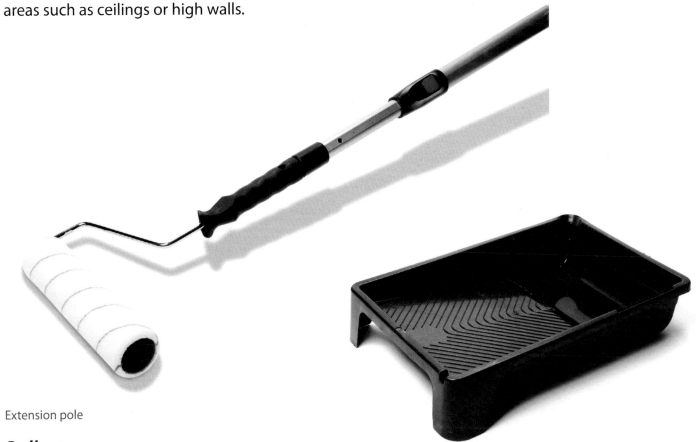

Extension pole

Roller tray

Roller tray

Roller trays are used to hold paint when using a roller. They are made from either plastic or metal and are designed to ensure even coverage of the roller sleeve with paint.

Scuttle

A **scuttle** is used to hold paint when using a roller from a ladder.

Scuttle

Definition

Relief materials – a material that has a pattern that stands out from the background

Did you know?

Some types of roller can be used as an alternative to the paste brush in order to apply paste to wall coverings

Paper hanging tools and equipment

Paper hanging is the technique of applying wallpaper to areas such as walls, ceilings etc. The term also includes the hanging of **relief materials**, fabrics and vinyl papers.

Brushes

Paste brush

Apart from being used to apply paste to wallpaper, a paste brush can also be used for washing down and sizing. They are available in a range of sizes between 100 mm and 175 mm.

Paste brush

Paper hanging brush

The paper hanging brush is also known as a sweep. It is used to remove all air bubbles between the wall covering and the surface to which it is being applied. After use, the brush should be cleaned in soapy water and hung up to dry.

Paper hanging brush

Measuring and levelling tools

Straight edge

Bevel-edged lengths of steel or wood provide straight edges and can also be used for several other activities such as, when used with a trimming knife (see below), producing butt joints and mitres when hanging wall coverings.

Straight edge

Spirit level

A spirit level can be used as a straight edge. It can also be useful when marking horizontal and vertical lines and can aid cutting of coverings before pasting.

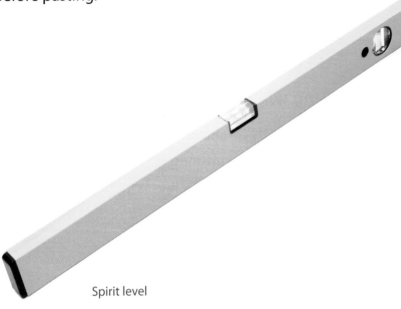

Spirit level

Plumb bob and line

A **plumb bob** is a weight to which string or twine is attached in order to produce a completely vertical line. These are still sometimes used instead of straight edges and spirit levels.

Plumb bob and line

Cutting equipment

Scissors or shears

Scissors or shears usually have polished stainless blades and are used for cutting or trimming wall coverings. Make sure they are kept clean and dry to prevent rusting. Scissors and shears must also be kept sharp or damage to wall coverings will result.

Scissors

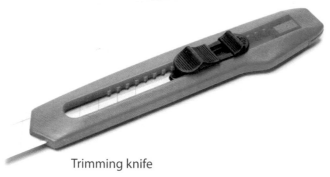

Trimming knife

Trimming knife

A trimming knife can be used as an alternative to scissors or shears but is most effective when used with a straight edge of some kind, i.e. a caulking blade or spirit level.

Casing wheel

Casing wheel

Casing wheels can have a serrated or plain blade and are used for trimming surplus paper around angles and obstacles such as light fittings and brackets.

Other types of paper hanging tools and equipment

Pasteboard

A pasteboard is a long sturdy table made from wood that can be folded down for easier transportation, either in the same location or between locations. It is used to support coverings during preparation, cutting and pasting. The pasteboard surface should be kept clean both during and after the work.

Pasteboard

Caulking blade

Caulking blades can be used as alternatives to paper hanging brushes when hanging fabrics or vinyl papers, but only on flat surfaces.

Caulking blade

Seam and angle roller

A seam and angle roller is used to roll down joints in wall coverings during hanging.

Seam and angle roller

Tape measure

Tape measure

A retractable metal tape measure is an important element of any decorator's toolkit. Available in a variety of lengths, most have both metric (centimetres and metres) and imperial (inches and feet) measurements. It is important to keep a tape measure clean as a dirty tape measure is likely to eventually clog up, making retraction of the tape back into the casing difficult.

Felt roller

Felt roller

Felt rollers are either a felt covered one-piece roller or several felt cylinders in line on a roller cage. They act as another alternative to the paper hanging brush.

Rubber roller

Rubber roller

Rubber rollers are used to hang very heavy materials, generally when a felt roller or paper hanging brush would not be heavy enough.

Pasting machine

Available as either table-top machines or as free-standing heavy duty pieces of equipment, a pasting machine makes applying paste to wall coverings easy. Paper is drawn through a paste trough which coats the backing of the wall covering evenly. Care must be taken when using these machines and you need to be aware that some delicate, decorative and other specialist coverings may be damaged if passed through a pasting machine. Always check the manufacturer's instructions.

Specialist tools and equipment

With the use of some special tools and some remarkably everyday items, it is possible to create some amazing decorative paint finishes, such as:

- graining – the imitation of wood

- marbling – the imitation of natural marbles

- broken colour – a multi-coloured effect

- stencil work – a cut-out pattern or design.

Creating paint finishes such as those listed above is now a separate and specialised division of the painting and decorating trade. Used mostly in the **restoration** of historic buildings, creating specialist paint finishes takes a lot of time to master but, if done well, can be extremely satisfying and rewarding.

For more information on the creation of specialist paint techniques and the use of some of the tools detailed below, see Chapter 9 Applying paint and creating special effects (page 191).

> **Definition**
>
> **Restoration** – returning a building to its original condition

Graining combs

Graining combs can be made from steel or rubber and are available with various teeth sizes and as different shapes to enable different types of grain effects.

Graining combs

Definition

Scumble – a semi-transparent stain or glaze applied over a hard, dry ground coat

Stippling brush

Stippling brushes are also available in various sizes and they are used to remove brush marks from **scumble** to give a stippled finish.

Stippling brush

Flogger

Flogging recreates the fine pore marks associated with wood by drumming on the surface with a long bristled brush – a flogger. The bristles of these brushes can be made from horse or hog hair.

Flogger

Mottler

A mottler is used to produce highlights and various other patterns in graining work.

Mottler

Overgrainer

An overgrainer is used in much the same way as a mottler and produces finer highlights in the graining work.

Overgrainer

Pencil overgrainer

Pencil overgrainer

A pencil overgrainer can be made from hog or sable and is used for figure work that creates depth. This brush creates an intricate secondary grain effect and is especially useful in the imitation of American walnut.

Drag brush

Drag brush

A drag brush is a coarse bristled brush made from horsehair, fibre or nylon. It is used to produce straight grained patterns.

Softener

A softener is used to soften and blend harsh edges of patterns. It is made from badger or hog hair and available in flat or round versions.

Softener

Sea sponge

Sea sponge

Sea sponges can be used to produce some of the best broken colour effects and softer patterned effects.

Veining horn

Veining horn

Veining horns are made from plastic and have one round end and one square end. They are used for reproducing the veins seen in many marbles and can also be used to produce oak grain patterns.

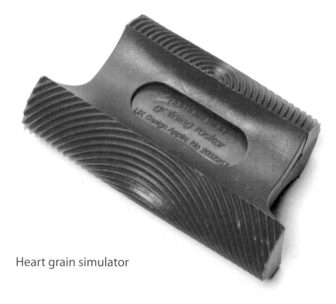

Heart grain simulator

Heart grain simulator

A heart grain simulator is a moulded rubber tool with a heartwood pattern imprinted on the face. It is used to produce the repeating heartwood patterns seen in various timbers.

Check roller

A check roller is used to reproduce the broken pore markings of various timbers. This tool is a combination of a mottler-type brush fitted to a series of serrated metal discs. The mottler provides the paint supply and the discs provide the pattern.

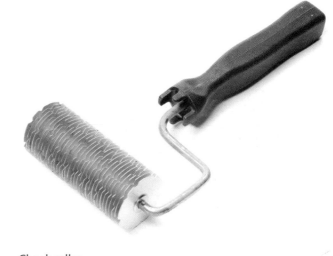

Check roller

Mahl stick

A mahl stick is a stiff rod made from timber or metal and is designed to support and steady the hand during signwriting and other work that requires a steady hand.

Mahl stick

Gilder's cushion, knife and tip

Gilding is the art of covering a surface with a very thin layer of gold. A gilder's cushion is a padded felt board covered in leather that is used when preparing and applying gold leaf. A shield is formed at one end using parchment which protects the gold and stops it from moving or being blown away. The knife and tip are used to cut and prepare the gold leaf (and sometimes other leaf).

Gilder's cushion, knife and tip

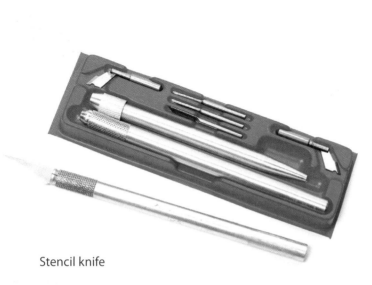

Stencil knife

The filling of a gilder's tip is made from squirrel or badger hair which is secured between two pieces of card. Before use, the filling has to be rubbed vigorously together in order to charge it with static electricity. The static then attracts the gold leaf to the tip, ready for application to the surface.

Stencil knife

A stencil knife is a tool used for cutting stencils out of stencil card or plastic.

Glazing tools and equipment

Safety tip

Always wear appropriate PPE when cutting glass (i.e. gloves and safety goggles)

Painters and decorators will sometimes have to replace small panes of glass and re-putty windows due to accidental breakages when decorating. The following tools and equipment are required for the replacement of glass.

Did you know?

Even though it is called glass cutting, the glass is not actually being 'cut' – it is being 'scored'. Scoring means making a deep scratch which weakens the glass and, when pressure is applied to the area, the glass breaks

Glasscutter

Glasscutter

Glasscutters have wooden or plastic handles and can have up to six small cutting wheels that can be rotated. Tips can be made from tungsten or have a diamond tip.

Putty or glazing knife

This tool is used to apply putty or stopper to small cracks and holes during the glazing process. It can also be used while forming the bevel finishes to putty used in glass replacement. The blade should be cleaned thoroughly after every task and checked regularly for any damage, which could result in imperfections in the surface of the finished putty.

Putty (or glazing) knife

Hacking knife

This is used for the removal of old putty. It can also be used with a hammer if required. It is advisable to retain the blade's sharpness with regular maintenance.

Straight edge and T-square

These items are used together to get straight edges and right angles when cutting glass.

Hacking knife

T-square

Did you know?

An old wood chisel can be used instead of a hacking knife

Glazing pliers

Glazing pliers

Glazing pliers grip onto glass when cutting it into thin strips.

Suction pads

Suction pads

Suction pads enable holding and carrying of panes of glass.

Tenon saw and mitre block

A mitre block has 45° cutting slots that help with the cutting of precise angles for beads on windows where putty is not used as the finish.

Tenon saw and mitre block

Pin hammer

Pin hammers are used to lightly tap in glazing **sprigs**.

Definition

Sprig – a very fine nail used in glazing

Pin hammer

Claw hammer

Claw hammer

Claw hammers are used to remove sprigs from hardened putty and, with the aid of a hacking knife, can also be used to remove putty.

FAQ

Will I need my own tool kit? If I do, how can I buy all the tools I need if I don't have much money?

While you are training, all the tools you need will be supplied by your training provider. When you have successfully completed your training, you may need your own tool kit, depending on who you work for. If you work for a large company, all tools and equipment are usually provided. If you work for a small company, they may not provide you with a tool kit. If you start your own business, you will definitely need to provide your own tool kit and equipment. It is a good idea to start a small collection of tools as soon as possible while you are training. You don't need to buy everything, but the essentials will always be useful. It is usually best to buy quality tools, which do cost a little more, but you will notice the difference.

On the job: Replacing glass

Stuart is a self-employed decorator and is currently working on a client's bungalow. He is removing the old and flaking paint from the bungalow's windows, making repairs and applying a new coat of paint. While Stuart is burning off the old paintwork with a LPG torch, a pane of glass cracks.

What PPE will Stuart need to replace the pane of glass? What specialist tools do you think he will need? Describe in a few words the procedure you would follow when replacing the glass.

Knowledge check

1. Name two pieces of equipment that can be used for removing surface coatings.

2. What different kinds of abrasive paper are available?

3. Draw a picture of a putty knife.

4. Why should you check electrical equipment before use?

5. What are the three parts of a paintbrush?

6. Name two types of roller.

7. What container can be used to hold paint when using a roller?

8. What is a pure bristle brush?

9. What could you use to paste wallpaper with instead of a paste brush?

10. What is the difference between a seam roller and a felt roller?

11. What is a sweep another name for and what is its use?

12. Why might a painter and decorator need a screwdriver?

13. What brush would you use to soften grain effects?

14. Name two tools that create highlights in graining work.

15. What is a veining horn used for?

chapter 5

Storage of materials, tools and equipment

OVERVIEW

There are many types of decorating materials, all of which present some often unique storage problems. This is because much of this material is coloured or patterned or in some other way produced for decorative effect. Any deterioration or damage will affect the finished result and may lead to the redoing of work. Tools and equipment must be stored with care in order to maintain their working condition. Health and safety considerations must also be taken into account. Guidance on manual handling can be found in Chapter 2 Health and safety.

In this chapter, we will cover:

- Storage of liquid material

- Storage of powdered material

- Storage of substances hazardous to health

- Storage of paper material

- Storage of decorating tools and equipment

- Storage of glass.

Storage of liquid material

Oil-based products

Oil-based products such as gloss and varnish should be stored on clearly marked shelves and with their labels turned to the front. They should always be used in date order, which means that new stock should be stored at the back with old stock at the front.

Oil-based products should be **inverted** at regular intervals to stop settlement and separation of the ingredients. They must also be kept in tightly sealed containers to stop the product **skinning**. Storage at a constant temperature will ensure the product retains its desired consistency.

Correct storage of liquid materials

Water-based products

Water-based products, such as emulsions and acrylics, should also be stored on shelves with labels to the front and in date order.

Some water-based products have a very limited shelf life and must be used before their use-by date. As with oil-based products, water-based products keep best if stored at a constant temperature. It is also important to protect them from frost to prevent the water component of the product from freezing.

Storage of powdered materials

Powdered materials a decorator might use include Artex®, fillers, paste and sugar soap.

Large items such as heavy bags should be stored at ground or platform level. Smaller items can be stored on shelves while sealed containers, such as a bin, are ideal for loose materials.

Powdered materials can have a limited shelf life and can set in high humidity conditions. They must also be protected from frost and exposure to any moisture, including condensation. These types of materials must not be stored in the open air.

Safety tip

Some larger bags of powdered materials are heavier than they first appear. Make sure you use the correct manual handling techniques (see Chapter 2)

Storage of substances hazardous to health

Some substances the decorator will work with are potentially hazardous to health, with **volatile** and highly flammable characteristics. The Control of Substances Hazardous to Health (COSHH) Regulations apply to such materials and detail how they must be stored and handled (see Chapter 2 Health and safety page 37 for general information about COSHH).

Definition

Volatile – quick to evaporate (turn to a gas)

Decorating materials that might be hazardous to health include spirits (i.e. methylated and white), turpentine (turps), paint thinners and varnish removers. These should be stored out of the way on shelves, preferably in a suitable locker or similar room that meets the requirements of COSHH. The temperatures must be kept below 15°C as a warmer environment may cause storage containers to expand and blow up.

Liquefied petroleum gas (LPG) must be stored in the open and usually in a locked cage. It should also be stored off the floor and protected from direct sunlight and frost or snow.

If flammable or explosive materials are to be kept in a storeroom, the room should be constructed in a very particular way. The floor should slope away from the storage area so that any spillages flow away and don't remain underneath the containers. The actual building should be constructed from concrete, bricks or another fireproof material. The roof should be made of an easily shattered material, which will minimise the effect of any explosion.

Doors on such buildings should be at least 50 mm thick and open outwards. Any glass used in the structure should be wired and not less than 6 mm thick. The standing area should have a sill surrounding it that is deep enough to contain the contents of the largest container stored.

The area should not be heated and should have safe electric switches and lights. Flameproof light switches should be on the outside of the store. The storage building should be ventilated at high and low levels and also contain two or more exits.

Naked flames or spark producing materials should be prohibited in the vicinity of the building, which should also be marked with red and white squares and clearly signposted as highly flammable.

The storage of LPG is governed by the Highly Flammable Liquids and Liquefied Petroleum Gases Regulations. Note that these regulations apply when 50 or more litres are stored, permission must be obtained from the District Inspector of Factories.

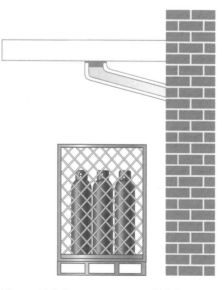

Figure 5.1 Correct storage of LPG

Storage of paper material

Wallpaper

Wallpaper rolls must be stored in racks with their ends protected from damage. They should also be stored in batches with their identifying number clearly marked. Rolls should be kept wrapped and protected from dust and they should never be in direct sunlight, which can result in fading of colours.

Some special wall coverings such as **lincrusta** have a shelf life that should be taken into consideration, ensuring that the oldest stock is used first.

Definition

Lincrusta – a wall-hanging with a relief pattern used to imitate wood panelling

Correct storage of wallpaper

Abrasive papers

Abrasive papers should be stored in packets that clearly identify them with respect to grade (most abrasive papers are labelled on the back with the grade of grit and thickness of paper). They should be stored on shelves ensuring that sheets are kept flat and rolls are stored upright or on reels.

Abrasive papers must be kept away from excessive heat as this makes them brittle. Dampness and condensation must also be avoided as it weakens glass papers and some garnet papers by softening the glue that binds the grit to the paper.

Storage of decorating tools and equipment

Dust sheets

Dust sheets should be folded neatly and stored on shelving. It is best to store clean sheets and dirty sheets separately in order to avoid contamination. Sheets must always be stored dry in order to prevent **mildew** attack and fabric fatigue (when fabric disintegrates in the hand like damp paper).

Brushes

Used brushes should be cleaned thoroughly and either hung up to dry or laid flat on well ventilated shelving. New brushes should be kept wrapped until they are needed. Mildew can grow on wet brushes that are not left to dry thoroughly, which can destroy the filling. Brushes that are stored for long periods without use should be treated with some form of insecticide to protect them from moth attack. Moth balls are ideal for this protection.

Rollers

After cleaning to remove all traces of paint and cleaner, roller sleeves should be hung up to dry in well ventilated areas. Mohair and lamb's wool sleeves will need extra consideration and you should always refer to the manufacturer's instructions.

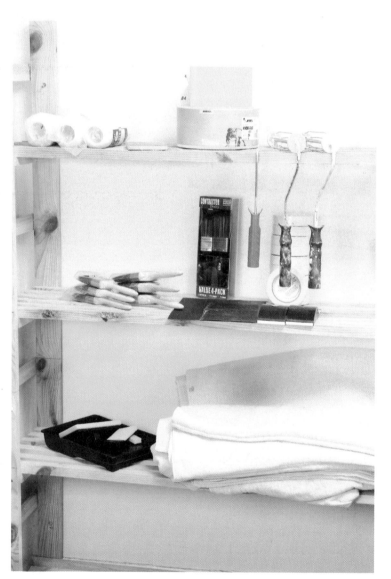

Correct storage of a variety of tools and equipment

Steel tools

Before storing, steel tools must be thoroughly cleaned and lightly oiled. A rustproof, oiled paper wrapping may be appropriate for long-term storage.

Storage of glass

There will be times when the decorator may be required to replace broken panes of glass and knowledge of the correct storage method is important.

Sheets of glass should always be stored vertically in racks and in dry conditions. If moisture is allowed to collect between the sheets they may stick together, resulting in difficult handling and possible breakage. Storage in dirty or dusty conditions can cause discoloration in the glass.

Remember

Look after your tools and they will look after you!

Remember

Always wear appropriate PPE when handling glass

If only a few sheets of glass are being stored, they can be leant against a stable surface

FAQ

How do I clean cotton dustsheets?

You will first need to shake the dustsheet to remove any loose dust, paint, wallpaper etc. You should then try and remove anything that is stuck to the dustsheet, such as pieces of wallpaper. Most cotton dustsheets can be washed in a washing machine at a low temperature, but always check the manufacturer's instructions. You can also take dustsheets to a laundry, although this is only worth doing if they are expensive heavy-duty dustsheets. After washing, dustsheets should be allowed to dry thoroughly before being folded and stored in a dry place.

Knowledge check

1. What is the best way to store powdered materials?

2. How should LPG be stored?

3. Name four substances hazardous to health. How should these generally be stored?

4. How should new brushes be stored?

5. What is meant by storing in date order?

6. What precautions should be taken in the area where explosive or flammable materials are to be stored?

7. How should wallpapers be stored?

8. What might occur if dustsheets or brushes are stored in damp conditions?

9. What should you do to steel equipment before storing?

10. How should glass sheets be stored?

chapter 6

Site preparation

OVERVIEW

Site preparation is what the decorator does before starting any work. Many items need to be protected before decorating is started, for example carpets, curtains and pictures and garden furniture and plant pots. Some items can simply be removed from the work area, however, this is not always possible and clearly when something is a permanent fitting (e.g. a banister or a radiator) it is impractical to move it.

This chapter will cover the following:

- Materials used to provide protection
- Common items requiring protection and methods used
- Protection of external items.

Materials used to provide protection

Safety tip

Make sure you use the correct manual handling techniques when lifting and moving items and use stepladders correctly when taking down pictures or covering light fittings. See Chapter 2 Health and safety (page 33) and Chapter 3 Working at height (page 67) for more information

Before any decoration is done, the most important task for the decorator is the protection of any areas, items, fixtures and fittings that are not being worked on that could be damaged.

Common items that need protecting include:

- carpets, rugs and other types of flooring
- sofas, curtains, chairs, tables, electrical equipment
- pictures, shelving, wall lights and sockets
- ceiling light fittings, shades and fire alarms/smoke detectors
- door furniture (handles, hinges, locks etc.)
- plant pots, garden seats and patio areas.

It is very important that, before you start any work, you look around and make sure that all items are protected by removing them or covering them with the appropriate material. Damage caused during decorating could be very costly, both to the decorator's pocket and reputation.

Dustsheets, tarpaulin and corrugated sheeting

Sheet materials such as dustsheets, tarpaulin and corrugated sheeting are the most commonly used and useful of protective materials. Sheeting can protect against paint and paste splashes and spillages and also small particles that are created when sanding or scraping.

Dustsheets

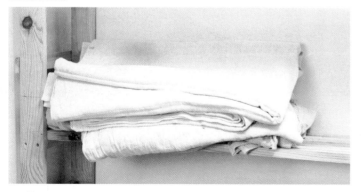

Dustsheets

Dustsheets of the highest quality should be used wherever possible as cheap alternatives do not always provide adequate protection. There are two basic types of dustsheet available, each with very different characteristics.

Cotton dustsheets

The best quality dustsheets are cotton twill sheets, which should be double folded to increase thickness. Cotton twill dustsheets are generally used to protect flooring and furniture and can be purchased in a variety of sizes, the most common being 4 m x 6 m. Other sizes are available and there are also special width and length dustsheets for use when working on staircases.

Advantages:

- present a professional image (when clean)
- when laid they remain in place well and are not easily disturbed when walked on
- available in different weights and sizes.

Disadvantages:

- expensive to purchase and clean
- heavy paint spillage can soak through the sheet
- can absorb chemicals such as paint stripper
- possible fire risk, especially if smoking is permitted in the workplace.

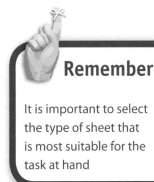

If laid well, a cotton dustsheet provides good protection

Polythene dustsheets

Polythene dustsheets can be used in the same way as cotton twill sheets, but they are waterproof and can be thrown away after use.

Advantages:

- inexpensive to purchase
- heavy paint spills do not soak through the sheet
- do not absorb chemicals such as paint strippers.

Disadvantages:

- do not present such a professional image as cotton dustsheets
- when laid they do not remain in place well and are easily disturbed.

Remember

It is important to select the type of sheet that is most suitable for the task at hand

Tarpaulin

Tarpaulin sheets are made of different types of material including:

- rubber-coated cotton
- heavy cotton canvas (usually very expensive)
- **PVC** coated nylon
- nylon scrim (coated with a polyester resin).

Definition

PVC – polyvinyl chloride (a tough plastic)

The most common size of tarpaulin sheets is 6 m x 4 m although larger sizes can be made to order. Because tarpaulin is protective against moisture, it is best to use it when washing down surfaces or when steam stripping wallpaper.

Tarpaulin sheeting is also used on and around scaffolding in order to give workers and the work area protection from bad weather conditions. It also offers protection to equipment and surfaces if there is a lot of movement around them.

Corrugated sheeting

Some work is aggressive and/or extensive (e.g. paint stripping to restore ceiling plaster), in which case the sheeting materials already discussed would not provide enough protection.

Corrugated PVC and cardboard can be purchased in sheet form and laid over the floor and jointed with 50 mm masking tape, offering more appropriate protection. Although this type of protection may be expensive to install, it helps avoid corrective work and undamaged sheets can be reused.

Other materials used for protection

As well as specially designed protective equipment, a decorator can use all manner of ordinary items in site preparation. Plastic bags, such as carrier bags or bin liners, are excellent for protecting light fittings, wall lights and chandeliers etc. The item is simply inserted into the bag, which can then be tied up and secured with masking tape – cheap and simple but very effective.

Masking paper and tapes are also used in the protection of items. Masking paper is a smooth brown paper and is used to protect floors, furniture and also windows. It comes on a roll in various width sizes from 150 mm to 450 mm. Masking paper can be held in place with masking tape but it is quite often self-adhesive.

Masking tape is often used to block off areas when painting, such as light switches, door handles and woodwork.

Cardboard boxes can be used to store smaller items such as pictures and ornaments. A small container, such as a box or a bag, can also be used to hold screws and nails that are collected when removing items and preparing the area (e.g. picture hooks, shelves, ventilation grilles etc.). This will ensure that nothing is lost or damaged.

Remember

Take care when handling items during site preparation – you will be responsible for any breakages you cause!

Common items requiring protection and methods used

As previously stated, you should always assess a work area for items that need to be protected before starting any work.

Figure 6.1 What do you think may need protecting in this room? See bottom of page for answers

Mirror, TV, TV stand, pelmet, curtains, glass (doors), rug, light switch, wall light, plug socket, ventilation grille, fireplace, mantelpiece, clock, candlesticks, carpet, skirting

Door furniture

Any items on an internal or external door, such as handles, finger plates, letter boxes, numbers, knockers, hinges, kick plates, push plates, door bell buttons, spy holes etc., are known as door furniture.

The easiest way to protect door furniture from paint, varnish or scratches is to remove it. To avoid the loss or accidental damage of any door furniture and screws, pack straight into a box or crate, covering individual items with newspaper, bubble wrap or something similar. Store the container in a safe and dry place.

If the removal of door furniture is impossible or inappropriate, covering it with masking tape is an acceptable alternative.

Safety tip

Site preparation can result in injury. Always be aware of hazards involved with the work you do such as slips, trips, falls and manual handling injuries

Some common examples of door furniture

Curtains and pelmets

Curtains should ideally always be removed before carrying out any work since cleaning, repair or replacement is usually very costly.

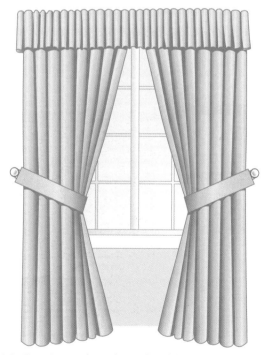

Figure 6.2 Curtains and a pelmet should ideally be removed

Remove curtains by first pulling them apart and then taking them off their track or pole. Next, carefully and neatly place the curtains into a plastic bag and remove them from the room, storing them safely in a dry place.

A pelmet is a piece of cloth or other material that covers the curtain pole or track. After it has been removed, cover it with a protective sheet or place it in a bag and again store in a safe dry place.

Curtain poles and tracks

Again, the best protection is to remove the item from the work area. Alternatively, the pole or track should be securely covered with a suitable material.

Figure 6.3 A wooden curtain pole

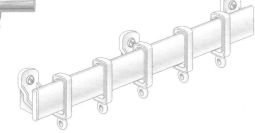

Remove the pole or track from its brackets, then unscrew the brackets from the wall. Place any small parts into a container to prevent them from being lost. All items should then be taken from the room and stored in a safe place.

Figure 6.4 A curtain track

Blinds

There are various types of blind, such as:

- roller blind
- vertical blind
- Venetian blind.

Roller blind

Before removal, the blind should be in a retracted or rolled-up position (where the window is visible). Next, remove the blind from its bracket and then unscrew the brackets from the wall. Place any small parts in a container and remove all parts of the blind from the work area.

Shelves

It is possible to work around shelving, but it is much easier to remove it. Removal also helps protect the shelving.

Wooden shelves can be easily removed, placed in a box or wrapped in protective material and moved out of the way. Glass shelving should be wrapped in newspaper, bubble wrap or other similar material to avoid breakage. Shelves are attached to walls with brackets, which are screwed on to walls with the aid of Rawlplugs™. Brackets and fixing screws should also be removed and put in a safe place.

FAQ

After a shelving bracket has been removed, how do I find the screw hole after wallpapering?

It is a good idea to place something in the hole as soon as you have finished sweeping over the paper. This could be a match or a screw.

Light fittings

These can be anything from wall lights to ceiling lights but may also include larger and heavier items such as chandeliers.

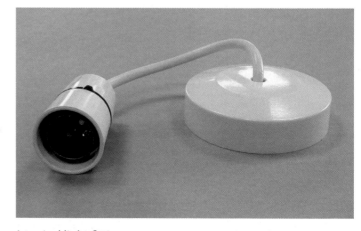

A typical light fitting

Only a qualified electrician should remove light fittings, although a decorator can remove light shades once the electricity has been turned off at the mains. The fuse must be removed from the mains fuse box or a warning notice put in place to prevent the power from being accidentally reconnected.

Fittings, once removed, should be wrapped and stored in a box or crate and kept in a safe location. Shades should be bagged and secured with tape. If chandeliers cannot be removed, they should be covered with light polythene sheeting and securely taped.

Mains fuse box

Covers and grilles

You may come across various types of covers and grilles used in ventilation, heating and air conditioning systems.

Made from plastic, metal and, in some instances, fibrous plaster, they can be found in various positions on walls throughout a building, providing cover for inlets and outlets.

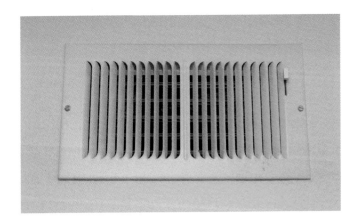

A typical ventilation grille

Remove by unscrewing. The cover or grille can then be stored in a safe place. If removal is inappropriate or impossible, a cover or grille can be covered with masking tape.

Remember

A decorator should never attempt to remove any kind of electrical fitting. If working on site, a qualified electrician should do this. If working in a client's house, the client needs to arrange for the fitting to be removed

Did you know?

Electricity on site should be reduced to 110 volts (this voltage reduces the risk of fatalities and serious injuries, but can still give a shock)

Furniture should be protected or removed

Furniture

This can be anything from a small coffee table to a dining table or a three-piece suite. Furniture also includes electrical equipment such as televisions, DVD players and stereos.

If possible, furniture should be removed from the work area to another room or a suitable temporary storage location. Where removal is not possible, furniture should be stored in a way that maximises the work space (e.g. moved to the middle of the room) and covered with suitable sheeting material depending on the type of work being carried out.

Carpets

Decorators are not usually qualified to remove or refit carpets. If necessary, removal and refitting should be arranged by the client.

Where carpets have not been removed a combination of dustsheets, polythene sheeting and masking tape should be used to protect them.

Ornaments, pictures and small valuable items

Wrapped in newspaper, bubble wrap or another suitable material, ornaments, pictures and valuables should be packed into containers such as crates or boxes. These should then be stored within the premises in a safe and dry place in order to protect them from damage, loss or theft.

Radiators

When working on new buildings, a decorator is able to carry out decorating tasks before radiators are fitted. Other situations may require the removal of radiators in order for certain work to be completed. If properly instructed in how to do so, a decorator may remove a radiator from a wall themselves. The following sequence should be followed:

1. Protect the area from leaks and damage.

2. Turn off the water supply.

3. Undo the radiator connections and drain (bleed) the radiator.

4. Remove the radiator from its brackets and store safely.

5. After decoration is complete, place and attach the radiator on to its brackets.

6. Reconnect the pipe work to the radiator.

7. Open the bleed valve.

8. Turn the water supply back on.

9. Close the bleed valve.

10. Check for leaks and leave the area clean and tidy.

There are three main types of radiator: panel, column and radiant panel.

Panel radiator

Protection of external items

When carrying out decorating tasks outside, it can be easy to forget about site preparation, but external items need protecting for the same reasons as internal items. External items that require protection include paths and patio areas, garden furniture, plant pots and alarm boxes. As with internal items, removal is the best form of protection, but where this is not possible, covering with an appropriate material is acceptable.

When you have finished decorating, always place items back in their original position. This will leave the client with a good impression of your workmanship so you will develop good relationships and benefit from customer recommendation.

Remember

Turn off the electricity/ water supply to wall heaters/radiators. This is as much to prevent harm to you as it is to protect the work area

On the job: Preparation

Arthur has been asked to strip the paint from and repaint the cast iron guttering and pipework at the rear of a client's property. Before Arthur begins the work, he looks around the part of the garden nearest the house. He can see a set of patio furniture, a bicycle lent against the house and clothes on a washing line attached to one of the external walls. There is also a variety of pot plants and shrubs on the patio near the house.

Before Arthur begins the paint job, what items and areas do you think he will need to protect? What is the best way to protect each of these items/areas? What safety precautions will Arthur have to consider? Think about things like the equipment and tools Arthur will use and the fact he will be working at height.

Knowledge check

1. What are good quality dustsheets made from?

2. Name an everyday object (i.e. one that doesn't have to be specially bought) that could be used for protection.

3. What is the voltage usually used on site?

4. Name three different types of radiators.

5. Name three different types of blinds.

6. What is the best way to protect flooring from damage?

7. Name four different pieces of door furniture.

8. Can you name the correct sequence of events for removing a radiator?

9. What assessment should you do before starting any work?

10. What special consideration should be taken account of when removing and storing electrical equipment?

chapter 7

Preparation of surfaces

OVERVIEW

Most surfaces that the decorator works with require some kind of preparation before work can begin. The correct preparation of a surface is essential if you are going to produce work that looks good and lasts well.

It is important that all surface contaminants such as dirt, oil, rust and loose or flaking existing coatings are removed. If contaminants are not removed, the ability of paint or paper to adhere (stick) to the surface will be affected.

This chapter covers:

- Defects

- Corrosion or rust

- Painted surfaces in poor condition

- Cleaning surfaces

- Abrading surfaces

- Special types of surface preparation

- Typical surfaces and their preparation

- Environmental considerations.

Defects

Before working on a surface, you will need to inspect the area for any defects. Surface defects include holes, cracks, dents and pitting and, if left, will affect the finished result. Correcting a defect is sometimes called 'making good' and just means the repair of a surface defect.

There is a wide range of substances that can be used to repair a surface defect and they generally fall into one of two categories:

* Filler – a smooth paste that is used to fill minor defects such as shrinkage cracks and nail or screw holes.

* Stopper – a similar material to filler but better for use on large holes and cracks.

Fillers and stoppers are both often referred to as 'filling agents' and this is how we will refer to them throughout this book.

Corrosion or rust

During your inspection of the work surface, you may notice areas where the surface has **corroded**, usually due to **rust**. This will have to be cleaned and removed before work can be carried out.

Removing rust by hand

Cleaning off rust by hand is hard work but is possible and is normally done when repainting rusty steelwork, as it is usually the cheapest method in the short-term. The problem with hand cleaning off rust is that the use of scrapers, chipping hammers, wire brushes and abrasives will not remove all traces of rust from the surface. In addition, the overuse of a wire brush can serve to only polish the rust on the surface, which can affect the ability of the primer to **adhere** to the surface.

Definition

Corroded – been destroyed or damaged by a chemical reaction

Rust – a red or yellowish-brown coating of iron oxide

Definition

Adhere (same as adhesion) – stick

The following procedure should be followed when cleaning by hand:

- Remove any traces of oil or grease to avoid spreading it around the surface.

- Scrape off all loose rust, **millscale** and previous coatings.

- Use a chipping hammer around rusted nails, bolts and rivets.

- Use a wire brush to remove loose rust, but avoid **burnishing**.

- Finish off by abrading with a rough aluminium oxide abrasive (P40 – P60) (see page 143 for more information on abrading).

Definition

Millscale – a scale that forms on steel

Burnishing – polishing

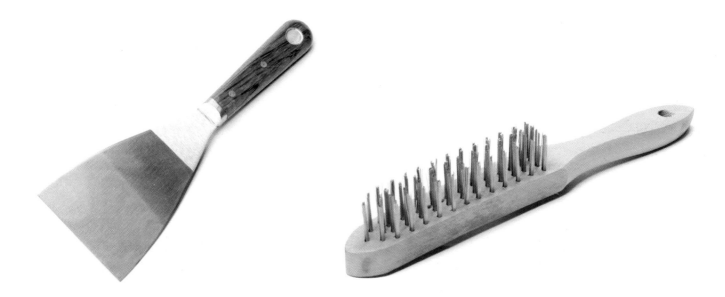

A paint scraper and wire brush can be used to remove loose rust

Removing rust with power tools

Power tool cleaning is generally quicker and more effective than hand cleaning and the life of the paint system will be extended by using this method.

Loose rust, millscale and the existing surface coating can be removed using power wire brushes, grinders and needle guns, although some millscale will not be removed even with power tools. Again, care should be taken not to over-polish the surface or the adhesion of the primer will be negatively affected.

The following procedure should be followed when cleaning with a power tool:

- Remove any traces of oil or grease from the surface.

- Scrape off all loose rust, millscale and previous coatings.

- Use a needle gun to remove rust around corroded nuts, bolts and rivets etc.

- Select the most effective method of removing rust to suit the nature and condition of the surface (e.g. rotary wire brush, disc sander or angle grinder).

Power tools such as needle guns and angle grinders can be used to remove rust from surfaces

Painted surfaces in poor condition

If the condition of the surface you are going to work on already has a coating of paint that is in poor condition (i.e. it has a brittle paint film or paint actually flaking off), it will be necessary to remove the entire paint coating in order to produce a good finished effect. This can be done using heat or chemical means.

Removing paint with heat

Removing paint by burning it off with heat, using either a LPG (liquefied petroleum gas) burning off torch or a hot air stripper, is the fastest method of removing coatings from timber surfaces.

LPG burning off torch

Advantages:

- this is a fast and efficient method of removing even thick layers of paint

- can be used when there is no mains electricity supply

- low running costs.

Disadvantages:

- many local authorities have banned the LPG burning off torch because of the fire risks involved

- there is a danger of cracking the glass in windows when working on the frames

- scorches timber easily.

Did you know?

Some local authorities have banned the use of LPG strippers in favour of hot air strippers. This is because there is a reduced risk of fire and damage to property

LPG burning off torch

Some important safety notes when using a LPG burning off torch

- When starting up, check the hose and fittings for gas leaks with a solution of detergent and water.

- Ensure that a fire extinguisher is nearby.

- Avoid burning off any timber adjacent to the roof structure of a building. This is because there are often birds' nests present or denatured timber, which can easily be ignited by the flame of a torch.

- Remove all curtains and furnishings when burning off around window frames.

- Always cease burning off operations at least one hour before you leave site and always carry out a final check for smouldering timber just before you go.

Hot air stripper

Hot air strippers

Whereas a LPG burning off torch uses a naked flame, a hot air stripper, as the name suggests, uses hot air to heat the paint, which can then be scraped off.

Removing paint with chemicals

There are two types of chemical paint remover: water-based (which comes in gel form) and solvent-based (which comes in paste form). Both types use chemicals to soften the paint coating, which can then be removed using hand tools such as shave hooks and scrapers.

Water-based paint remover

Water-based paint remover is the one most commonly used in the trade.

Advantages:

- can be used as an alternative to burning off with heat (so suited to areas where risk of fire or heat damage is high)
- doesn't scorch or damage the surface
- can be used on most types of paint.

Disadvantages:

- water-based paint removers raise the grain of timber
- slow and messy
- expensive
- can soften some plastic surfaces
- all traces of the paint remover must be cleaned from the surface after scraping off the paint. If any remains, future coatings may be damaged
- the chemicals in the paint remover and the fumes produced can be harmful to health.

Safety tip

Paint fumes give off toxic gases when burnt so make sure you are wearing the correct PPE

Safety tip

Always wear the appropriate PPE when using chemical paint remover (gloves and goggles)

Solvent-based paint remover

This type of paint remover is very good at removing thick layers of paint (up to 3 mm thick) from many different types of surface such as fibrous plaster, timber, stone, marble, brick and cast iron. The paste should be applied thickly to the surface (between 3 and 6 mm thick) with a trowel or filling knife.

The paint remover can then be covered with cling film or greaseproof paper to prevent the solvents from evaporating and improve their action (sometimes referred to as a poultice after a type of medical dressing). The paint remover can be left to act on the surface for periods ranging from two hours to five days, depending on the type and thickness of the coating being removed:

- thin layers of paint – two to three hours
- thick layers of paint – overnight
- very thick layers of paint – two or more days
- ornamental mouldings such as plaster cornices or ceiling roses may have to be left for up to five days.

Advantages:

- same as for water-based paint remover
- if left for the correct period of time, no scraping is necessary and the paint remover can just be washed off, making it ideal for delicate surfaces that cannot be scraped.

Disadvantages:

- expensive
- the process can take a long time
- all traces of the paste must be removed from the surface after the paint has been taken off. The surface will also have to be neutralised with water (to stop the chemicals from continuing to work).

Definition

Spot primed – the application of primer (base coat) to small areas

Cleaning surfaces

After a surface has been sufficiently repaired, it has to be cleaned in preparation for decorating. You may find that the surface you are to work on is in good condition (also known as sound), and will not need any repair, but even sound surfaces can have patchy areas where the existing coating has peeled off or is flaking. In these situations, before you can clean the surface, the flaking paint has to be removed to form a solid edge. The bare areas then need to be **spot primed**. When the primer has dried, the edges of the repaired area can be surface-filled with a suitable filling agent.

Cleaning the work area is the next stage in surface preparation. Various substances such as dirt, grease and everyday grime can contaminate a surface without it looking like the area is dirty. You may also find that substances such as tar from cigarette smoking will need to be removed from ceilings and other surfaces.

When washing a surface down, it is very important that the correct washing agent is used. Dirt can be removed with sugar soap or a mild detergent and elbow grease (i.e. scrubbing with a brush!). Oily and greasy marks will probably only come off with the use of white spirit or turps, applied to the surface with a cloth or brush. Make sure that the area is thoroughly rinsed after cleaning and allowed to completely dry.

When working on some types of building, such as hospitals, a special cleaning contractor may be brought in to wash surfaces down due to possible health risks.

Did you know?

Tar from tobacco smoking affects the adhesion of paint to a surface and can bleed through emulsion paint

Safety tip

Always wear appropriate PPE when cleaning a surface and make sure you read the product safety information. Most cleaning agents can remove natural oils from the skin, which can cause skin conditions such as dermatitis

Abrading surfaces

Abrading a surface means wearing away the top layer by rubbing (i.e. creating friction). This is a very important part of surface preparation and provides a **key** for the coating or covering to be applied and smooths the surface in order to give a good quality finish.

It is important that the correct type of abrading material is used:

- An abrasive that is too rough can leave scratches on surfaces that show through to the finish.

- An abrasive that is too fine can result in preparation time taking longer than necessary and may be ineffective at removing or levelling rough surface imperfections.

- Cheap, inadequate abrasives such as glass paper can greatly extend the preparation time of any job because they tend to get blunt and clog very quickly.

Abrading materials

Abrasive materials fall into two broad categories:

- wet and dry abrasives

- dry abrasives.

Wet and dry abrasives

Wet and dry abrasives can, as the name suggests, be used in both wet and dry conditions. A waterproof adhesive fixes the abrasive particles to the backing, which means that the paper doesn't lose the particles when it gets wet – in fact, if wet and dry paper is used dry, it tends to clog up and so is more suited to wet use.

Did you know?

When washing a surface, you should always start at the bottom and work upwards. This avoids streaking of painted surfaces, which can damage the finish

Definition

Key – roughness on a surface provided to aid adhesion

Remember

Always choose the correct type and grade of abrading material for the surface and the job

The aggregates (abrasive particles) used in wet and dry abrasive paper have traditionally been silicon carbide, but aluminium oxide is now becoming increasingly popular. The particles of aggregate are closely grouped together and are referred to as being 'closed coated'. Water, or sometimes mineral oil, can be used as a lubricant, which prevents the paper from becoming clogged. Wet and dry abrasive paper is available in grades from P80 (coarse) through to P1200 (very fine).

Advantages:

- extremely good for high-quality work
- wide range of grades available
- cleans the surface as it abrades
- low dust levels.

Disadvantages:

- more expensive than dry abrasives
- unsuitable for bare timber
- clogs up easily if used dry
- the surface has to dry before it can be decorated.

Dry abrasives

This is an abrasive that uses a non-waterproof adhesive to fix the particles of abrasive to the backing paper. The aggregates used in this type of paper have traditionally been glass and garnet, but they are very poor when compared with aluminium oxide grit, which is now used extensively on dry abrasives.

Aluminium oxide abrasive, sometimes referred to as production paper, is usually available 'open coated', where the particles of aggregate are spaced apart on the backing paper. This reduces the risk of clogging as the gaps between the aggregate particles allow waste to escape. A dry powder lubricant can be used on some types of dry abrasives, which breaks away when heat is generated by the abrading process, preventing clogging of the abrasive.

Advantages:

- Aluminium oxide papers are available in grades ranging from P20 (coarse) through to P320 (very fine).

- When aluminium oxide wears down, particle edges shear off revealing another smaller but sharper edge (see Figure 7.1).

- Available in sheet, roll, disc and belt form.

- Also available in self-adhesive rolls so that the abrasive can be torn off and then fixed to a purpose-made rubbing block.

New abrasive

Aluminium oxide particles wear down and break away

Remaining particles are smaller and sharper

Figure 7.1 How aluminium oxide breaks down

Disadvantages:

- Aluminium oxide abrasive paper can be expensive, but when compared with other abrasives it is more economical in the long-term.

- High dust levels.

Grades of abrasives

We have already briefly touched on the range of grades available but it is important you know what a grade is. A grade that gives a coarse abrading effect will have large particles and therefore less of them. Figure 7.2 shows aggregate on a P20 grade dry abrading paper where only 20 particles of aggregate will fit on to a 25 x 25 mm area.

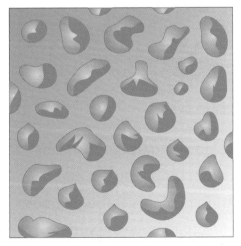

Figure 7.2 A small number of large aggregates will give a coarse abrading effect

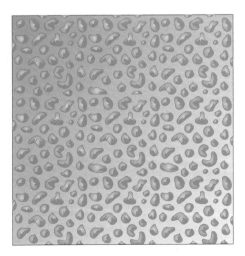

Figure 7.3 A large number of small aggregates will give a fine abrading effect

A grade that gives a fine abrading affect will have lots of small particles. Figure 7.3 shows aggregate on a P80 grade dry abrading paper where 80 particles of aggregate will fit on to a 25 x 25 mm area.

It is important to select the correct grade of abrasive for each job. The incorrect use of abrasive can either affect the finished appearance of the work or increase the time spent on preparations. The grade can be found printed on the back of an abrasive paper and relates to the particles of aggregate to every square 25 mm.

Mechanical sanding

Abrading material attached to an electrical tool can greatly reduce the time spent preparing surfaces and increase the surface area covered. Electrical sanders work by moving an abrasive pad or belt at a fast speed and some models are equipped with a convenient dust collection bag.

Belt, drum and orbital sanders

The heavy duty sanders most commonly used by a decorator are belt, drum and orbital sanders.

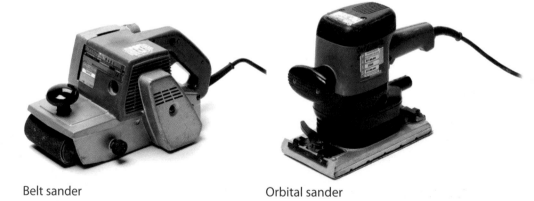

Belt sander

Orbital sander

Drum sander

Belt and orbital sanders are hand-held power tools best used for sanding large, flat items of joinery. A drum sander on the other hand is self-propelled and used for stripping floors. A rough grade of abrading material should be used first to remove the surface coating. The rough surface can then be brought up to a smooth finish by progressively using finer and finer abrading material.

> ### Safety tip
> Abrading will create dust particles so ensure adequate ventilation of the work area and wear appropriate respiratory PPE

Advantages:

- effective at abrading large areas
- mechanical sanders have a faster rate of abrasion than abrading by hand.

Disadvantages:

- more expensive than abrasive papers
- only suitable for work on large, flat areas
- can create large amounts of dust.

Small electric sanders are also available with triangular heads for use when sanding corners.

Disc or rotary sanders

Rotary sanding involves the use of rotating discs of abrasive material and can be used to prepare small or contoured surfaces.

Different types of abrasive disc are available:

- flat discs that require a backing pad
- flap discs made up from flaps of abrasive, which are more expensive but also more effective
- grinding discs that can be used for removing very heavy, small areas of rust.

Advantages:

- do not burnish the surface
- relatively low initial cost of equipment
- effective at removing isolated patches of rust.

Disadvantages:

- only suited to small areas
- not suited to complex surfaces (discs cannot reach into awkward corners).

Safety tip

Do not use an electrical sander near the power socket which it is plugged in to. For example, if you are sanding a skirting board near a power socket, plug the sander in to another power socket. This will avoid the risk of electric shock if you accidentally damage the plug or power cable

Did you know?

Abrasive discs can be fitted to electric drills and angle grinders

Disc (or rotary) sander – in this instance, an electric drill fitted with an abrasive disc attachment

If the electrical sander you are using is equipped with a dust collection bag, make sure it is working and empty before using the tool. After you have finished sanding, the wood dust collected should be disposed of appropriately. Sanding dust should not be left in bags indoors as there is a danger of spontaneous combustion (sudden bursting into flames).

See Chapter 4 Tools and equipment (page 90) for additional information on abrading equipment.

Special types of surface preparation

Safety tip

Knotting solution is highly flammable and so should not be exposed to naked flames. You must also make sure you wear the appropriate PPE when handling this material

Some surfaces may need special preparation in addition to the methods already discussed in this chapter.

Timber knots

During the preparation of timber surfaces, you may notice knots in the wood. A knot is a place in the timber where a branch was joined to the tree. If you were to paint bare timber without preparing the knots first, you may find that sap bleeds from the knot staining the paint finish. A material called knotting solution is available that can be applied to areas where the wood is knotted in order to seal it.

Knotting solution can also be applied to areas of timber that have been stained with resin, tar splashes, felt pen and biro marks – again, the knotting solution will stop the stains bleeding through the paint. The main ingredient in most knotting solutions is shellac which is produced by an insect and melted into thin flakes.

A knotting bottle will prevent knotting solution from evaporating and drying out. Make sure the surface is clean and dry before applying the knotting solution with a brush. It should dry quite quickly, after which time the surface coating can be applied.

Knotting bottle

Stain sealing

Shellac is also available coloured (known as pigmented shellac). Aluminium provides a silver pigment whilst titanium provides a white pigment and these are very effective stain sealers especially on:

- stains made by fire and smoke

- water stains

- previously creosoted timber.

Pigmented shellac can even seal pet, smoke and fire odours (smells).

Alkaline surfaces

The chemical nature of surfaces such as concrete, cement rendering, asbestos sheeting and some plasters is **alkaline**. This can cause problems if a solvent-based paint system is to be applied because the alkalinity in the surface can attack the paint rather like a paint stripper, causing a paint defect known as **saponification**.

To prevent saponification, it is necessary to apply an alkali-resistant primer, which forms a barrier between the surface and the paint. Acrylic surface coatings are resistant to alkalis, so you would think an alkali-resistant primer wouldn't be needed, however, their **permeable** nature allows any alkalinity through if the surface becomes damp.

Did you know?

Shellac is not only used in stain sealers. It can also be used as a safe coating on food such as fruit and sweets to give them a glossy shine

Definition

Alkaline – having a pH greater than 7 (an acid has a pH of less than 7)

Saponification – a chemical reaction that makes soap and so foams up as a result

Permeable – allowing things to pass through

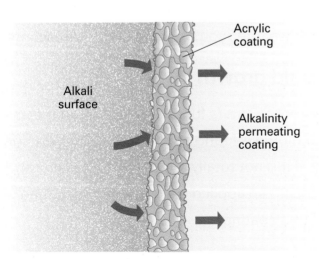

Figure 7.4 Alkalinity permeating through an acrylic coating

Friable surfaces

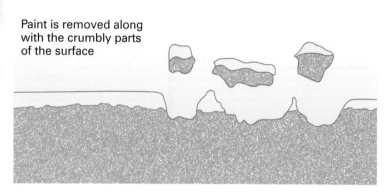

Paint is removed along with the crumbly parts of the surface

Figure 7.5 Paint applied to a friable surface

A friable surface is one which crumbles away easily when you rub your hand over it. Examples of this kind of surface include weathered cement rendering or old, weathered brickwork (known as spalled). If paint is applied to a friable surface, it won't last very long as it will come off with the crumbly parts of the surface.

In order to get around this problem, a stabilising solution can be applied before the paint. The surface should be brushed down first with a stiff brush, which will remove any loose particles. The stabilising solution can then be applied, which soaks deep into the surface acting like a glue, binding it down. A good paint finish can now be achieved.

Porous surfaces

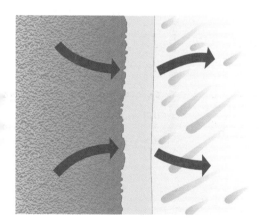

Figure 7.6 Silicone water repellent used on porous brickwork

A porous surface is one that contains tiny holes through which liquids or gases can pass. In order to prevent porous surfaces, such as brickwork, from being penetrated by water or damaged by frost, a silicone water-repellent layer can be applied, which waterproofs the surface and protects it. It dries clear and unless you compared it with an untreated surface during wet weather, you wouldn't know it was there.

Surfaces affected by mould growth

Mould is a furry growth of micro-organisms (a fungus), which often grows in moist and warm conditions. If mould is found during surface preparation, all traces of it must be removed. If it is not totally removed, the mould can quickly re-establish itself underneath an applied coating, which can then lead to the premature failure of that coating.

The following procedure should be followed to remove mould growth:

- Wet the mould to avoid the spread of spores to other areas.

- Remove heavy patches of the mould with a scraper or wire brush.

- Apply a fungicidal wash to the affected area and allow it to dry.

- If possible, the affected area should be left for a week or so and re-treated if the mould reappears.

Mould growth

In most cases only one application will be necessary. This is because fungicidal wash has a residual effect on the surface, which means that traces of it remain, continually removing mould growth from the surface, sometimes for many years.

Surfaces affected by wet rot

Wet rot is a growth of brown fungus that can occur in damp timber, such as that in window frames. As the fungus grows, it destroys the wood and the only long-term treatment of wet rot is the removal of moisture from the timber. Before you can work on an area affected by wet rot, you must treat it using the following procedure:

- Rake out any defective timber using a scraper, shave hook or chisel. Allow the surface to dry out if possible and flood the exposed timber with a clear wood preservative. Allow it to dry and spot prime the affected areas with wood primer.

- Fix wood screws (non-ferrous, i.e. non-iron) into the timber.

- Apply a coat of two pack polyester filler to the surface and allow to dry. The screws will help the filler adhere to the surface.

- Apply a second coat of filler and allow to dry. Use abrading paper to rub down the filler so it is **flush**. It may be necessary to use an acrylic spot filler (a soft putty) to fill any minor imperfections.

Safety tip

Fungicidal washes are poisons and should be treated with extreme care. PPE must be worn at all times, i.e. rubber gloves, goggles and suitable overalls. After using this type of product, make sure that you wash your hands before eating or smoking

Definition

Flush – when one surface is level and even with another surface

Find out

Why should you not put iron screws into timber affected by wet rot?

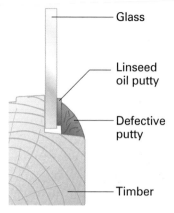

Figure 7.7 Defective putty

Glass

Linseed oil putty

Defective putty

Timber

Defective putty

During the removal of old paint from window frames, some of the putty is likely to break away. After other surface preparations have been completed, the bare timber can be primed and any defective putty replaced with linseed oil putty.

Any old putty that has not broken away, will be firmly adhered to the window frame and will not need to be replaced. You may, however, notice a gap between the old putty and the glass. This gap must be completely sealed by forcing in linseed oil putty using a putty knife. See Figure 7.7.

Bonded asbestos

Asbestos is a fibrous mineral that was used as a form of insulating material, especially from the 1950s to the mid-1980s. We now know that asbestos particles, when they are breathed into the lungs, can cause lung cancer and a disease called asbestosis. These diseases can kill, which is why since 1999 it has been illegal to use asbestos in construction, except for some very exceptional reasons.

Bonded asbestos is where the asbestos is bonded in cement and it usually comes in corrugated sheet form and was commonly used for garage and shed roofs as well as pipes and guttering. Although bonded asbestos is not thought to present significant risks to health, it should still be handled with care. Never use any dry abrading methods – instead, if you have to abrade the surface to remove mould or dirt, always use a wet abrasion method. This will avoid the release of potentially harmful dust particles.

Before work starts on a site, it must be inspected for asbestos. However, if you think you have discovered the fibrous form of asbestos, stop work IMMEDIATELY and tell your supervisor. If tests reveal that the material is asbestos, specially trained teams will then be brought in to deal with its removal or stabilisation. No one can work with asbestos unless they hold a special licence issued by the Health and Safety Executive. Remember, be alert – your actions now could make you seriously ill in years to come.

Safety tip

If you are working on a bonded asbestos surface, make sure you take precautions and wear the correct PPE, i.e. gloves and a face mask

Did you know?

There are three different types of asbestos known as blue, brown and white, although they CANNOT be identified by their colour. Blue and brown asbestos are much more dangerous than white asbestos, but all of them should be treated as potential risks to health

Plasterboard

Plasterboard is plaster sandwiched between two boards and is used for interior partition walls and ceilings. The two boards are actually only a stiff lining paper and so will soak up moisture. By applying a hard waterproof coating to the plasterboard before applying surface coverings such as wallpaper, the wallpaper will not bond with the plasterboard surface and the plasterboard will not be damaged when the wallpaper is removed.

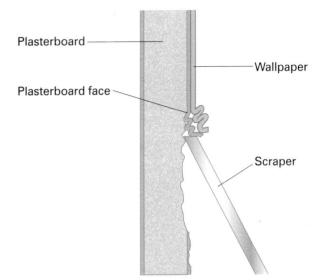

Plasterboard

Plasterboard face

Wallpaper

Scraper

Figure 7.8 Plasterboard damaged during wallpaper removal

Figure 7.8 shows plasterboard being damaged by the removal of wallpaper which has been applied without first applying a waterproof coating.

Surfaces affected by efflorescence

Efflorescence is the appearance of white patches on cement-based surfaces and can occur on brickwork, rendering and internal plaster. Because cement is porous, (look back at page 150 to remind yourself about porous surfaces) moisture such as rain can penetrate the cement, dissolving some of the lime creating calcium hydroxide. The calcium hydroxide rises to the surface when the cement dries out and, once all the moisture has disappeared, calcium carbonate is left on the surface as the white patch we can see.

Efflorescence

Although efflorescence will eventually disappear on its own, if a surface is to be decorated, any efflorescence will have to be removed during preparation. The treatment for surfaces affected by efflorescence is removal by scrubbing with a stiff fibre brush or a wire brush. Never try and remove efflorescence by washing the surface as the calcium carbonate will simply dissolve in the water and sink back into the cement.

Defective rendering

Rendering is a coating of plaster applied to stonework and during your assessment of this type of surface, you may notice cracks in the rendering.

There are several different methods of filling in these cracks and the most commonly used methods are as follows:

For small cracks:

- Scrape away any loose coatings and particles of masonry.

- Apply filling agent – exterior grade filler (polyfiller type) could be used but this would probably re-crack after a short period of time, whereas exterior acrylic caulking will provide more permanent flexible repair.

For large cracks:

- Rake out and undercut the crack using a 25 mm scraper or pointing trowel (see Figure 7.9 and 7.10). Fill the crack with a sand and cement mortar to a ratio of one part cement to three parts soft sand (see Figure 7.11). This action is known as 'pointing up' and when dry it can be painted over, but this repair would probably re-crack after a short period of time.

- Alternatively, rake out, undercut and fill as above and then allow to dry. Apply a bituminous caulking compound over the crack and bed a nylon type bandage over the length of the crack. Further applications of the caulking compound can then be made over the bandage to provide an invisible reinforced repair, which will last longer than the first method described.

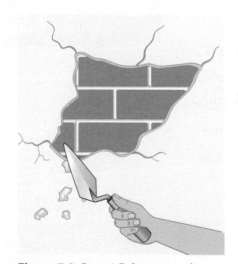

Figure 7.9 Step 1 Rake out any loose coatings and rendering

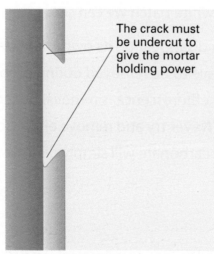

Figure 7.10 Step 2 Undercut the crack

The crack must be undercut to give the mortar holding power

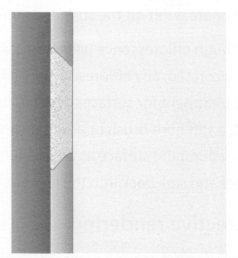

Figure 7.11 Step 3 Point up the crack with mortar

Caulking

Caulk is a waterproof filler and sealant and is used in cracks and gaps. Mastic is an acrylic type of caulk and is applied using a mastic gun, which is a frame that holds and helps dispense mastic from its tube. When dry, mastic feels a bit like rubber.

A mastic gun is easy to use, but the process of filling a crack is often done incorrectly. In order to caulk correctly, the bead of applied caulk must be wiped off with a wet finger, after which surplus caulk can be removed with a filling knife. Any remaining material can then be sponged off.

Figure 7.12 shows two examples of how caulking can be applied to the tops of skirting boards. The illustration on the left shows the caulk applied correctly. The illustration on the right shows incorrect application.

Caulking with a mastic gun

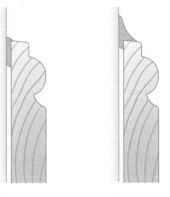

Correct   Incorrect

Figure 7.12 Correct and incorrect caulking

Painting an already painted surface

Before painting over an already painted surface, it is important that you carry out a simple test to find out how well the old layer of paint is adhered to the surface. If it is not strongly adhered to the surface, there is little point painting over it as your finish will not last very long. Figure 7.13 illustrates how to perform the 'scratch test', which can be performed on most surfaces as part of the preparation process.

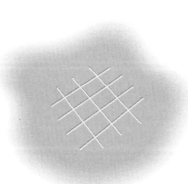

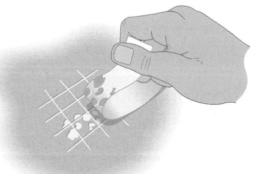

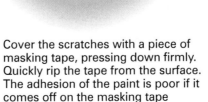

Use a sharp Stanley knife to make a few cuts in one direction and a few cuts in the opposite direction

Cover the scratches with a piece of masking tape, pressing down firmly. Quickly rip the tape from the surface. The adhesion of the paint is poor if it comes off on the masking tape

Figure 7.13 The scratch test

Typical surfaces and their preparation

By now, you have learnt that surface preparation is a very important task and that if you prepare a surface thoroughly, you will end up with a high-quality finish and a good reputation. You have also read about a number of different preparation processes. Over the next few pages we will look at some typical surfaces you may find yourself working on during your career, along with appropriate preparation tasks for each.

New softwoods/hardwoods

Abrading a new softwood or hardwood may result in damage due to scratching or furring (the lifting of wood fibres). For this reason, it is best to simply dust off the surface prior to painting. If you notice any raised nail heads, they will need to be punched down below the surface and filled with a suitable filling agent prior to painting.

Rough sawn timber

Rough sawn timber should be dry brushed thoroughly to remove soil, vegetation and dust.

New plaster and plasterboard

New plaster and plasterboard should be dry scraped with a scraper to remove any bits and nibs and then dusted down. Never abrade the surface as this would scratch it.

Brickwork, stonework, rendering, pebbledash and concrete finishes

These types of surface can be thoroughly cleaned with scrapers and dry brushing in order to remove dirt and powdery residue. The surface may need to be scrubbed if efflorescence is present or washed if mould is present, but it should be allowed to dry thoroughly before being worked on. Dusting off should be carried out prior to painting.

Remember

Take care when scrubbing with a wire brush so as not to damage surfaces with scratches

Ferrous metalwork

Ferrous metals contain iron and include cast iron, wrought iron, mild steel and stainless steel. These surfaces are prone to rusting and will need to be cleared of all rust prior to painting. Depending upon the extent of the rust, it can be removed with the use of a wire brush, mechanical wire brush, abrasive papers and/or scrapers.

New metalwork needs to be cleaned down with white spirit or an emulsifying agent to remove grease and oily residues.

Remember

The over-burnishing of rust when preparing steelwork results in reduced adhesion of metal primer

Non-ferrous metalwork

Non-ferrous metals do not contain iron and include aluminium, zinc, copper and brass. These should be dry and free from grease prior to painting. Previously painted non-ferrous metals need to be abraded and any rust deposits found should be scraped back to a firm edge where any flaking paint is evident.

Painted wood

Painted wood should be washed down using sugar soap and warm water, then rinsed with clean water. The surface should then be abraded to provide a key and then dusted down to remove surface dust.

Painted plaster

Wash the surface down with sugar soap and warm water, then rinse off with clean water and abrade the surface. Repair any indentations, cracks, holes etc. with a filling agent. Areas filled should be sanded down once dry and dusted off ready for painting.

Did you know?

Common defects on plastered surfaces include blistering, flaking, peeling and mould growth

Plastic

Plastic surfaces might include guttering and down pipes. Although, normally, plastic guttering and down pipes are used because they are virtually maintenance-free, there may be occasions when a client wants a colour change. Special primers are required for preparing plastic surfaces to receive paint finishes, as good adhesion is hard to achieve. Plastic surfaces should be degreased and abraded to provide a key before application of the primer.

Glazed tiles

These should be washed down using a detergent, for example sugar soap.

Polystyrene tiles

Polystyrene tiles should be dusted off and filled with a plaster-based filler where any damage is evident. Oil-based fillers should not be used because they will dissolve the polystyrene.

New wallpaper

Wallpapered surfaces, including those covered with embossed and blown vinyl paper, should be dusted off and any paste marks washed off before painting.

Old wallpaper

Old wallpaper is best stripped off using either water and a scraper or a steam stripper and a scraper. Some papers, such as vinyl, can be peeled off, leaving the backing paper on the surface.

Environmental considerations

It is pointless preparing and painting a surface if it is damp or weather conditions are wet or very cold as this will affect the paint finish or its ability to dry. These are environmental considerations and must be taken into account during surface preparation.

Damp surfaces

We have already looked at how a dirty and greasy surface can affect decorating, but a damp surface can also cause problems. Wet, unseasoned timber or wet, newly plastered or washed walls must be given an adequate drying out period. Applying any kind of surface coating or covering before the surface is totally dry will result in any of the following:

- blistering

- peeling (due to lack of adhesion)

- discoloration

- staining.

Cold or wet weather conditions

Decorating in cold conditions (below 5°C) or wet weather can result in the following:

- failure of water-based paints to dry (due to lack of adhesion)

- washing off of water-based paints

- blooming of alkyd finishes (i.e. loss of gloss and a cloudy surface)

- rain pitting of alkyd finishes

- peeling.

FAQ

What is lead paint and why is it dangerous?

Some older houses and buildings, usually built before 1960, may have surfaces that are decorated with paint containing lead. Lead is a soft, heavy metal that can be hazardous to health if breathed in or swallowed. Years ago, even though the health risks were well known, lead was sometimes added to paint to speed the drying and give the paint protective properties. During your training, you will learn about the precautions to take when dealing with lead paint, but as some general advice, remember: always wear PPE, including a face mask and goggles; never burn off lead paint with a LPG torch or gun; don't rub down the surface with dry abrasive paper. Finally, you will not be able to tell from looking whether or not paint contains lead. As a general rule, on older properties, treat all paint as if it is lead-containing paint.

Knowledge check

1. What is a disadvantage of removing rust by hand?

2. What surface preparation process can result in burnishing and why should this be avoided?

3. Name two different methods of removing paint.

4. Suggest a substance you could use to remove oily and greasy marks from a surface.

5. Explain what a key is.

6. What tends to happen if wet and dry abrasive paper is used dry?

7. When would you use knotting solution?

8. What could you apply to a surface to seal a stain or an odour?

9. How could you prevent saponification on an alkaline surface?

10. What might happen if you don't get rid of all mould growth on a surface before you decorate it?

11. What is wet rot and what does it do?

12. What should you do if you think you have discovered asbestos?

13. What happens if you try to remove efflorescence by washing it away?

14. How could you prepare a rendered surface that had both small and large cracks?

15. What might happen if you decorate in wet weather or cold conditions below 5°C?

chapter **8**

Surface coatings

OVERVIEW

Applying a surface coating can be one of the cheapest, quickest, easiest and most effective tasks a decorator will perform. A variety of surface coatings such as varnish, wood stain and paint can preserve, protect and decorate a surface. A decorator can also put their creative skills to good use, producing interesting and attractive effects if requested.

This chapter will cover:

- What are surface coatings?
- Applying coatings to various surface types
- Paint defects.

What are surface coatings?

Surface coatings are applied in order to:

- Protect – steel can be prevented from corroding due to rust and wood can be prevented from rotting due to moisture and insect attack.

- Decorate – the appearance of a surface can be improved or given a special effect (e.g. marbling, wood graining).

- **Sanitise** – a surface can be made more hygienic with the application of a surface coating, preventing penetration and accumulation of germs and dirt and also allowing easier cleaning.

- Identify – different colours or types of surface coating can be used to distinguish areas or components (e.g. pipework identified using the British Standards Institution's colour coding system).

Surface coatings generally fall into one of the following categories:

- Paint

- Varnish

- Wood stain

- Sealers and preparatory coatings.

Paint

Paint is either water-based or solvent-based. Water-based paint means that the main liquid part of the paint is water. Solvent-based paint means that a chemical has been used instead of water to dissolve the other components of the paint (see below for more information on the components of paint). When paint is applied to a surface, the water or the solvent (depending on the type of paint) evaporates into the air leaving the other components behind on the surface.

Until recently, solvent-based paints were the number one wall coating choice for plaster, masonry and other surfaces, but changes in safety and

Definition

Sanitise – to make something clean and free of germs

Safety tip

Solvents used in solvent-based paints are usually toxic and highly flammable so take proper precautions when using them

environmental legislation have forced manufacturers to develop water-based products as safer alternatives to solvent-based paints.

Water-based paints are now widely used on both internal and external surfaces that were traditionally the strict domain of solvent paint systems.

The components of paint

Paint is a liquid material that changes into a solid material when it dries, forming a decorative and protective film on a surface. You could say that the liquid part of paint is only temporary and is a way of getting the other components on to the surface.

Paint consists of three components:

1. Thinner – this is either the water or solvent part of the paint that dissolves the other components and makes them suitable for surface application. When paint is applied to a surface, the thinner evaporates totally as it dries.

2. Binder – this is a **resin** and forms the film of the paint. The binder also determines the performance of the paint (how long it lasts) and the degree of gloss (shine).

3. Pigment – the colour. Pigment is also responsible for the paint's opaqueness (the ability to cover the underlying surface). Some pigments, in paints such as primers, also influence the performance of the paint, for example rust-inhibiting pigments prevent the formation of rust.

Definition

Resin – this can be either natural (produced by plants and trees) or man-made (plastic)

Watching paint dry

Not the most exciting thing to do, but the process of paint drying is quite complex and it is useful that you understand the basic principles. Paints dry in one of two ways:

1. Air-drying – the thinner (the water or solvent) evaporates (see Figure 8.1a). You may become aware of this during the paint application,

for example when brush applying oil-based gloss to a large surface, you may find that the coating becomes difficult to brush, indicating that the thinner is evaporating.

2. Chemical reaction – drying either happens as the paint reacts with oxygen in the air (a process known as oxidation) or as ingredients in the paint that have been kept separated in the solvent combine on the surface to create a film (a process known as coalescence). This reaction can also be heat-activated. See Figure 8.1b.

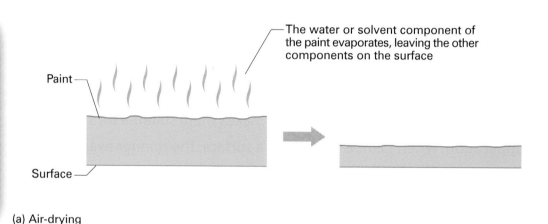

The water or solvent component of the paint evaporates, leaving the other components on the surface

Paint

Surface

(a) Air-drying

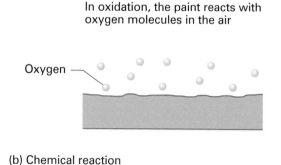

In oxidation, the paint reacts with oxygen molecules in the air

Oxygen

(b) Chemical reaction

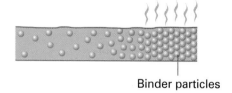

In coalescence, as the liquid part of the paint evaporates, the binder particles are drawn together, causing them to fuse and bind the pigment into a film

Binder particles

Figure 8.1 The paint drying process

Air-drying paints are usually single pack paints and are supplied in one container. Paints that dry using a chemical reaction (which are usually special purpose paints, such as floor paints and corrosion-resistant coatings used on structural steel) are supplied in two packs. One pack contains the base (Part A) and the other pack contains the hardener (Part B). They are kept separate so that the chemical reaction that causes the paint to start drying only happens when they are mixed together. Once two-pack paint is mixed together, it must be used within about four hours, after which the consistency becomes unworkable. The amount of time two-pack paints remain at a workable consistency is known as the **pot life**.

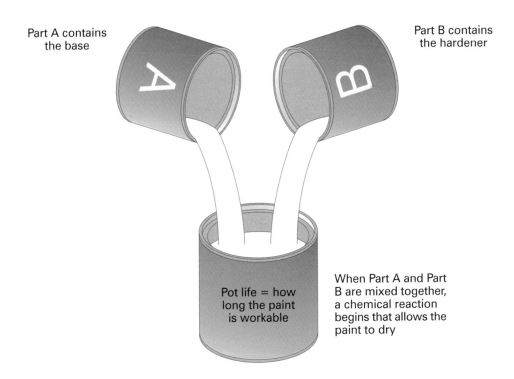

Part A contains the base

Part B contains the hardener

Pot life = how long the paint is workable

When Part A and Part B are mixed together, a chemical reaction begins that allows the paint to dry

Figure 8.2 Part A and Part B of a two-pack paint

If two-pack paint is not used up within its pot life period, expensive mistakes can be made:

- If too much paint is made up (mixed together), it will set in the tin resulting in an expensive waste.

- If application equipment, such as brushes, rollers and spray equipment, is not cleaned in good time it could be ruined.

Special attention should be paid to any safety information provided with paints. Some types of paint contain chemicals known as isocyanate groups. These chemicals give off vapours (gases), which irritate the airways (windpipe and lungs) and could cause conditions such as asthma. You should also avoid contact with the skin or eyes. The correct PPE should be worn when working with these materials, including air-fed masks and powered respirators. In addition, make sure the area you are working in is well ventilated and take regular breaks.

Good painting practice

Successful painting is dependent on a number of factors:

- Preparation
- Environmental conditions
- Film thickness
- Workmanship.

Preparation

The importance of proper surface preparation prior to painting cannot be over-emphasised. No surface should be painted unless it is in a sound, firm, clean, dry condition. (For more detailed information on surface preparation, see Chapter 7 page 135.)

Environmental conditions

Environmental conditions refer to the dampness or wetness of the surface and the temperature of the surface and the surrounding atmosphere. Wet timber and wet plaster are obvious examples of surfaces that cannot be painted successfully. They must be allowed to dry out thoroughly before painting can be attempted.

Weather conditions affect the drying time and finish of paint films and are especially important when working on an outdoor surface. Warm, dry conditions accelerate drying. Cold and humid conditions **retard** drying and can detrimentally affect the finish of gloss paints, causing them to dry flat or 'bloom' (develop a cloudy white film on the surface).

Paints should not, therefore, normally be applied during cold or humid conditions, or just before these conditions can be expected.

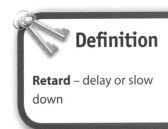

Definition

Retard – delay or slow down

Film thickness

On new surfaces, it is necessary to apply an initial paint film build-up of adequate thickness. This can usually be achieved by the application of at least three coats of solvent-based systems, such as one coat of primer, one coat of undercoat and one coat of gloss. Alternatively, at least two coats of emulsion and acrylic water-based paints can be used, all applied at the correct spreading rate as indicated for the specific product. The use of an additional coat, sometimes of primer, undercoat or finishing paint, is often also beneficial.

Workmanship

Good workmanship is a very important factor in good painting practice. Site and surface preparation may seem like boring and time-consuming jobs, but if corners are cut, your work will be of a poor quality and your reputation as a good decorator will soon suffer.

Water-based or solvent-based paint?

These two types of paint protect surfaces in different ways. Solvent-based paint, such as alkyd gloss, protect surfaces by forming a waterproof layer. This keeps out any moisture, preventing the formation of wet rot in timber surfaces.

Water-based paints protect surfaces by providing a moisture screen that prevents most of the water from penetrating the surface. Any moisture that does penetrate is allowed to escape as water vapour through the **permeable** coating.

Most water-based paints do not have the ability to soak into the surface of timber, which means that they do not stick as well as oil-based paints. Solvent-based gloss is sometimes used over water-based acrylic undercoat, but its performance is marred by the lack of adhesion of some water-based coatings.

There are products on the market that have managed to combine the adhesion of solvent-based paints with the flexibility of water-based coatings and these are known as solvent-based acrylics.

Definition

Permeable – having openings that liquids and gases can pass through

Primers

A primer is the first coat of paint applied to a surface. If the surface preparation for the priming coat or the application and choice of the primer is incorrect in any way, the durability of the paint system will be reduced.

Some manufacturers market their primers as 'universal', which means that they are intended for use on a wide range of surfaces. However, these primers should not be expected to out-perform those primers specifically designed for a particular surface. For example, when painting on an aluminium surface, a two-pack etch primer designed specifically for use on aluminium would be a far better primer than a universal primer, which is listed as being suitable for use on non-ferrous metal.

The main purpose of a priming coat is to make the surface suitable to receive further coats of paint. See Table 8.1 on page 181 for further information on primers.

Undercoats

Undercoats, or intermediate coats as they are sometimes called, are designed to provide a sound base for the finish coats by providing:

- opacity (the ability to cover and hide the underlying coating)
- adequate film build for protection and finish quality.

Ordinary oil-based undercoats can become brittle with age, thus reducing the performance of the finishing paint system. Water-based undercoats are best used as part of a full water-based system and do not perform well under solvent-based paints, particularly on exteriors.

For further information on undercoats, see Table 8.1 on page 181.

Finishes

A finish is the topmost layer of paint – the one that will be seen. Matt and silk emulsions are the most commonly used type of finish on interior wall and ceiling surfaces. Matt emulsion is smooth, non-reflective (i.e. not glossy), quick-drying and available in countless colours. Silk emulsion is washable and gives a sheen finish when dry. It is ideal for areas such as kitchens and bathrooms. Vinyl soft sheen is a modern subtle alternative to vinyl matt and silk emulsions, drying to a soft mid-sheen and suitable for most wall and ceiling surfaces.

For more information on matt and silk vinyl emulsion finishes, see Table 8.1 on page 182.

Eggshell finishes are durable paints suitable for interior use, particularly conditions of high-humidity such as kitchens and bathrooms. It is optional whether or not eggshell paint is stirred before use. Unstirred, the paint has a semi-gel consistency that doesn't drip from the brush but liquefies on application. Alternatively, the paint can be beaten to a full-bodied fluid consistency, which is recommended for roller or spray application.

The standard finish used to protect joinery components is a gloss finish. The most common type used is alkyd gloss.

Alkyd gloss

Alkyd gloss paint is solvent-based and is usually used over a solvent-based alkyd undercoat. The advantages of alkyd gloss paint include:

- good covering power (with the exception of strong yellows, reds and oranges)
- it provides a good waterproof barrier
- it provides a durable, easy-clean, high-gloss finish
- it is available in a wide range of colours.

Did you know?

Water-based eggshell paints are becoming more popular than oil-based eggshell paints because they do not give off strong fumes

The disadvantages of alkyd gloss paint include:

- white alkyd gloss is prone to yellowing, or chalking, and loses its gloss on exteriors after a number of years

- it becomes brittle with age, which means that it is prone to cracking and flaking when it can't accommodate any movement in the timber surface

- the waterproof nature of the finish prevents any water trapped within the surface from escaping, which can lead to blistering of the paint system or even wet rot.

Water-based gloss

Water-based gloss is made from acrylic polymers and is fast becoming an alternative to traditional solvent-based gloss due to legislation and environmental issues. Water-based gloss is sometimes labelled 'microporous' which means it is permeable. Permeable paints are said to let the surface 'breathe', which means that the small holes in the coating allow air to reach the surface.

Advantages of water-based gloss paint:

- easier to apply than alkyd gloss

- provides a flexible, non-yellowing film

- does not give off toxic fumes when drying

- equipment can be easily washed out in water after use

- dries quickly in dry, warm conditions

- resistant to alkalis

- does not chalk upon ageing.

Disadvantages of water-based gloss paint:

- does not provide a high-gloss finish

- does not provide a seal between the glass and putties on timber window frames

- drying can be retarded by cold, damp conditions and it can freeze, both on the surface and in the can, due to its water content

- can be washed off exterior surfaces by rain while still wet

- not as resistant to abrasion as alkyd gloss.

Varnish

Varnish is a transparent finish that is applied to wood. It comes in matt, satin and gloss varieties and provides a tough water- and heat-resistant protective coating. The components of varnish are as follows:

- drying oil – this is a substance such as linseed oil, tung oil or walnut oil, which dries to form a hardened solid film

- resin – yellow-brown resins such as amber, copal or rosin are used in many varnishes

- thinner or solvent – white spirit or paint thinner is commonly used as the thinner or solvent.

Table 8.2 on page 184 gives some information about some of the types of varnish available.

Wood stain

Wood stain is a type of dye, which when applied to timber soaks deep into the fibres and emphasises the grain of the wood. Available in a variety of colours and suited to either indoor or outdoor purposes, wood stain can transform bare timber surfaces into beautiful shades of natural wood. Quite often, wood stain does not offer any protection to a surface, it simply colours it.

Remember

Because varnish is transparent (see-through), careful preparation of the wood surface is very important, as any faults or defects will be clearly visible

Always check the type of stain you are using and seal the wood with a varnish or polish after staining if necessary.

For more information on wood stain, see Table 8.3 on page 186.

Sealers and preparatory coatings

Sealers and preparatory coatings are substances that are applied to a surface in order to prepare it to receive subsequent surface coatings. Sealers, such as knotting solution, act by sealing in the surface material, thus preventing anything from leaking out of or into the surface. Preparatory coatings are special substances that protect and preserve the surface from things such as water, mould, rust or alkali surface coatings. Applying a suitable and appropriate sealer or preparatory coating to your surface before decorating it, will preserve the surface and ensure a high-quality, long-lasting finish.

Table 8.4 on page 188 gives information about some common examples of sealers and preparatory coatings.

Applying coatings to various surface types

Bare untreated timber

- Seal any knots in timber using knotting solution.
- Prime the surface using oil-based wood primer (for external surfaces) or acrylic primer undercoat (for internal surfaces).
- Fill using polyfiller and decorator's caulk.
- Rub down and dust off.
- Apply one coat of undercoat.
- Rub down and dust off.
- Apply another coat of undercoat if necessary.
- Apply one coat of gloss.

Alternatively, for staining or varnishing tasks:

- Fill holes in timber with putty or coloured stopper.

- Apply basecoat.

- Rub down and dust off.

- Apply one coat of woodstain or varnish.

- Lightly rub down and dust off.

- Apply second coat of woodstain or varnish.

Previously painted timber

- Rub down using sandpaper.

- If necessary, fill using polyfiller or caulk.

- Apply one coat of undercoat.

- Rub down undercoat and dust off.

- Apply one coat of gloss.

Rough cut timber

- Apply one coat of timber preservative or wood stain.

- Apply second coat of timber preservative or wood stain.

Untreated plaster board

- Apply one coat of emulsion thinned by up to 20%.

- If necessary, fill using polyfiller then lightly rub down and dust off.

- Apply one coat of emulsion.

- Rub down and dust off.

- Apply second coat of emulsion.

Did you know?

Newly plastered walls can be painted with emulsion because they allow the wall to 'breathe'

Bare plaster

- Dry scrape with a scraper or broad knife.

- Apply one coat of alkali-resisting primer or one coat of emulsion thinned by up to 20%.

- Fill any holes or dents using polyfiller then rub down using sandpaper and dust off.

- Apply first coat (eggshell or emulsion).

- Rub down and dust off.

- Apply second coat of paint (eggshell or emulsion).

Previously painted plaster

- Wash down using sugar soap solution.

- Fill any holes or cracks using polyfiller and decorator's caulk then rub down.

- Dust off.

- Apply first coat (eggshell or emulsion).

- Rub down and dust off.

- Apply second coat of paint (eggshell or emulsion).

Artex

- Apply one coat of emulsion thinned by up to 20%.

- Apply one coat of emulsion.

- Rub down and dust off.

- Apply second coat of emulsion.

Steelwork

Previously painted

- Dry abrade using emery paper or a scraper and wire brush to remove any rust.

- Dust off.

- Apply good general purpose metal primer or zinc phosphate to areas where rust has been removed.

- Apply undercoat.

- Lightly abrade and dust off.

- Apply gloss coating.

Previously unpainted

Same procedure as for previously painted, but using a full coat of primer rather than spot priming or touching up.

Metal surfaces

Ferrous metals (iron and steel)

- Remove all corrosion and millscale via mechanical means.

- Degrease with white spirit if necessary.

- Allow the surface to dry thoroughly.

- Apply primer with a brush.

- **Bitumen**-coated surfaces will require sealing with quick-drying primer sealer.

- Four coats of paint will be required to achieve adequate film thickness (as recommended by the British Iron and Steel Association).

Did you know?

Ferrous metals rust; non-ferrous metals do not rust

Definition

Bitumen – a heavy, semi-solid, brown-black substance created as a result of the oil refining process (also known as asphalt or tar)

Non-ferrous metals (aluminium, copper, zinc, brass etc.)

- Degrease surface with white spirit.

- Galvanised and zinc-sprayed surfaces should be treated with **mordant solution**.

- Etch the surface with wet and dry abrasive paper and white spirit to provide a key.

- Apply one coat of metal primer or universal primer.

Masonry

- Clean the surface with a jet wash or scrub with a suitable detergent, remove loose materials and treat any efflorescence.

- Any mould, mildew, algae or lichen should be treated with a sterilisation wash before being removed with a scraper or stiff brush. The surface should then be re-treated with the sterilisation wash.

- Ensure surface is completely dry before applying any coating.

- Prime new masonry and older or weathered masonry with stabilising solution or all-purpose primer, applying with a brush. Previously painted surfaces in good condition may not need priming.

- Subsequent coatings can be applied by brush, roller or spray.

Definition

Mordant solution a substance that provides a key

Did you know?

The reason the first layer of primer applied to masonry should be applied with a brush, is because the action of brushing forces the paint into the surface

Surface coating defects

During your career as a painter and decorator, there may be occasions when the surface coating you have applied fails in some way. This may be because you did not adequately prepare the surface prior to applying the coating, because the environmental conditions (e.g. the weather) were not favourable or because your tools or materials were of poor quality.

Find out

Look at each surface coating defect detailed in Figure 8.4. How can each defect be prevented?

Figure 8.3 shows some common types of surface coating defect and how they might be caused. Familiarise yourself with these defects and do everything possible to prevent them from occurring.

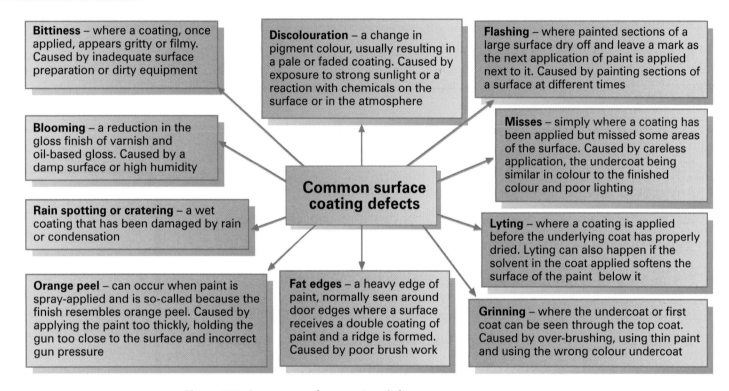

Bittiness – where a coating, once applied, appears gritty or filmy. Caused by inadequate surface preparation or dirty equipment

Discolouration – a change in pigment colour, usually resulting in a pale or faded coating. Caused by exposure to strong sunlight or a reaction with chemicals on the surface or in the atmosphere

Flashing – where painted sections of a large surface dry off and leave a mark as the next application of paint is applied next to it. Caused by painting sections of a surface at different times

Blooming – a reduction in the gloss finish of varnish and oil-based gloss. Caused by a damp surface or high humidity

Misses – simply where a coating has been applied but missed some areas of the surface. Caused by careless application, the undercoat being similar in colour to the finished colour and poor lighting

Common surface coating defects

Rain spotting or cratering – a wet coating that has been damaged by rain or condensation

Lyting – where a coating is applied before the underlying coat has properly dried. Lyting can also happen if the solvent in the coat applied softens the surface of the paint below it

Orange peel – can occur when paint is spray-applied and is so-called because the finish resembles orange peel. Caused by applying the paint too thickly, holding the gun too close to the surface and incorrect gun pressure

Fat edges – a heavy edge of paint, normally seen around door edges where a surface receives a double coating of paint and a ridge is formed. Caused by poor brush work

Grinning – where the undercoat or first coat can be seen through the top coat. Caused by over-brushing, using thin paint and using the wrong colour undercoat

Figure 8.3 Common surface coating defects

Surface coating defects can occur before the coating is even applied to the surface. Most defects that occur in the tin are normally caused by:

- incorrect storage

- incorrect mixing

- the coating going past its use-by date.

Common defects of coatings in the tin include:

- Settling – where the components of the paint (see page 163) become separated because of long-term storage.

- Skinning – where the coating forms a skin. The skin can usually be easily removed and the surface coating used as normal

- Fattening or livering – where paint has thickened to such an extent that the adding of a solvent or oil does not thin it. This defect can also occur when the wrong solvent or thinner has been used or when the paint is past its use-by date.

FAQ

Why is oil-based paint usually called 'alkyd paint'?

Oil-based paint and alkyd paint are not the same thing. Alkyd paint is a *type* of oil-based paint. Some oil-based paints are made from natural oils and resins, whereas alkyd paint is made from synthetic materials, but it is still oil-based.

What is a spreading rate?

The term 'spreading rate' refers to the amount of surface area a surface coating will cover per litre. Some surface coatings will have a high spreading rate (for example, 18 square metres per litre), while others will have a lower spreading rate (for example, 10 square metres per litre).

On the job: Knotting solution

Charlie is a final-year apprentice and is working on a new build property. He is working with Dave who is an experienced painter and decorator. They have just started work on the property and as part of his surface preparation, Charlie gets out a knotting bottle. He is just about to start treating the knots on some timber when Dave tells him 'not to bother'. Dave tells Charlie that treating the wood with knotting solution is a waste of time, and he should just prime all the timber instead.

Do you think treating timber with knotting solution is a waste of time? What do you think Charlie should do?

Knowledge check

1. Name four reasons why a surface coating might be applied.

2. What happens to the water or solvent component of paint when it is applied to a surface?

3. Name three things the pigment in paint might be responsible for.

4. Briefly describe what happens when paint dries via chemical reaction.

5. How might weather conditions affect a surface coating's drying time?

6. What is a universal primer and why might you choose to use one?

7. What two things does an undercoat provide?

8. What is the most commonly used paint finish on interior walls and ceilings?

9. What are the three components of varnish?

10. Why might you apply wood stain to a timber surface?

11. Briefly describe the procedure you would follow if applying surface coatings to a bare plaster wall.

12. How many coats of paint does the British Iron and Steel Association recommend are applied to ferrous metal surfaces?

13. Name three reasons why a surface coating might fail.

14. What is lyting?

15. How are most surface coating defects that occur in the tin caused?

Table 8.1 Paint – primer, undercoat, finishes (vinyl emulsions)

Acrylic wall primer *A water-based alkali-resisting paint made from high-quality pigments and a tough acrylic resin; air-drying and water-based*	**Uses** Primer is the first coating applied to a wall and provides better adhesion of paint to a surface, increases the durability of subsequent coatings and also serves as a protector **Special properties** Low odour, fast-drying, easily applied, good opacity and flow; can also contain ingredients that cover most stains **Colour range** Various **Pack sizes** 2.5 litres to 10 litres **Spreading rate** Between 10–12 square metres per litre on smooth, non-porous surfaces **Drying time** In normal conditions it dries in four to five hours **Equipment cleaner** Water **Storage** Replace lid firmly; protect from frost **Surface preparation** Ensure the surface is sound, clean and dry **Application** Stir well before use and apply one full coat in even strokes using a brush or roller, ensuring the primer is applied firmly to the surface
Undercoat *A dense covering made from lead-free pigments bound-in by a durable alkyd resin; air-drying and solvent-based*	**Uses** The coating applied to a surface after the primer but before the finish. Suitable for both interior and exterior surfaces **Special properties** Easy to apply, excellent opacity with good flow and levelling characteristics; provides a smooth, well-bound surface for finishes **Colour range** Various **Pack sizes** 750 ml, 2.5 litres and 5 litres **Spreading rate** Approximately 17 square metres per litre on smooth, prepared surfaces

	Drying time 16 to 24 hours
	Equipment cleaner White spirit or turpentine substitute
	Storage Replace lid firmly; store away from heat and flame
	Surface preparation Ensure surface is sound, clean, dry and completely free from grease. Previously painted surfaces should be rubbed down with wet abrasive paper to provide a good key. Bare surfaces should be primed with the appropriate primer. After priming, fill cracks and nail holes with filler
	Application Stir well before use. Apply one or more coats of undercoat as required with a brush or roller. Give each coat 16 to 24 hours to dry thoroughly, then rub down lightly to remove any nibs before applying gloss finish. If there is a lengthy time between undercoat and gloss application, another coat of undercoat will be required before applying gloss finish
	Restrictions None
Vinyl emulsions *Available in matt or silk varieties, easy to apply and suitable for the decoration of most interior walls and ceilings; air-drying and water-based*	**Uses** Both matt and silk emulsions are the number one choice for most domestic internal surfaces. Matt emulsion is best suited to surfaces where a shine is not desired, particularly those that are uneven or have imperfections. Silk emulsion leaves an attractive sheen when dry and is more durable and washable than matt emulsion
	Special properties Easy to apply, high opacity, resistant to yellowing and fading
	Colour range Huge
	Pack sizes 1 litre, 2.5 litres, 5 litres and 10 litres

Spreading rate Approximately 14 square metres per litre for matt and approximately 12 square metres per litre for silk, depending on surface porosity and texture

Drying time Under normal conditions, touch-dry in one hour; can be recoated after two to four hours

Equipment cleaner Water

Storage Replace lid firmly; protect from frost

Surface preparation Attend to all surface imperfections and cracks. Prime and undercoat as necessary. Previously gloss painted surfaces will need to be rubbed down thoroughly to provide a good key

Application Stir well before use and apply with a brush or roller. When the paint is to be applied to absorbent surfaces, thin the first coat with clean water. Further coatings can be applied un-thinned. Two coats are normally recommended for a good film build, although a third coat may be necessary with severely contrasting colour changes. For spray application, thin with clean water as required, up to approximately 10% by volume of water to paint. Do not apply when the air or surface temperature is below 5°C. Conditions of high humidity can prolong the drying time

Table 8.2 Varnishes

Quick-drying varnish	**Uses** Good for the protection and decoration of interior bare wood surfaces and previously varnished surfaces in good condition.
A fast-drying high-quality varnish made from a special acrylic resin; air-drying and water-based	**Special properties** Fast drying time, low odour, easy application
	Colour range Clear (gloss and satin finishes)
	Pack sizes 750 ml and 2.5 litres
	Spreading rate Approximately 12 square metres per litre, depending on the porosity (number of pores) of the timber
	Drying time Under normal conditions, touch-dry in one hour; hard dry after four hours
	Equipment cleaner Water
	Storage Replace lid firmly; protect from frost
	Surface preparation Surfaces must be sound, clean and dry. Sand lightly along the grain of the timber; do not use wet abrasive paper at this stage as this could cause staining later on if used on dry timber
	Application Apply an initial coat of the varnish by brush. The initial milky-white appearance will disappear to a clear, virtually invisible film as the varnish dries. Leave to dry for approximately one hour under good drying conditions then lightly sand along the grain to remove any raised fibres. Apply as many coats as required to fill the grain (usually three coats), allowing 30 minutes between coats. Rubbing down can then be carried out with wet abrasive paper, using water as the lubricant. Rinse the surface and allow to dry

	Restrictions As quick-drying varnish is water-based, it should not be applied when the ambient temperature is below 5°C or in conditions of high humidity. For clear wood treatments, it is essential to take all possible precautions against contamination by iron, any trace of which can cause unsightly stains. Do not use wire wool for rubbing down
Quick-drying floor varnish *A high-quality, low odour, fast-drying varnish; water-based*	**Uses** Suitable for all bare and pre-treated interior timber floors **Special properties** Durable and fast-drying **Colour range** Clear gloss and clear satin **Pack sizes** 2.5 and 5 litres **Spreading rate** Approximately 18 square metres per litre, depending on the nature and porosity of the timber **Drying time** Under normal conditions, touch-dry in one hour; can be recoated in two to four hours **Equipment cleaner** Water **Storage** Replace lid firmly; protect from frost **Surface preparation** Ensure surface is sound, clean and dry. Rub down previously varnished or stained surfaces with fine wet abrasive paper and mild soapy water, then thoroughly rinse and allow to dry. Do not prepare the surface with wire wool **Application** Stir well before use and apply evenly with a brush or roller along the grain. Use only a glass or plastic container to hold the varnish and avoid contact with ferrous metals while wet. On new surfaces, the first coat should be thinned with up to 10% clean water, followed by at least two further coats of undiluted varnish. Avoid contact with alcohol and harsh chemicals. Do not apply when air or surface temperatures are below 5°C. Conditions of high humidity will prolong the drying time

Table 8.3 Wood stain

Protective wood stain *A specially formulated protective wood stain made from UV light-absorbing pigments and water-shedding resins; air-drying and solvent-based*	**Uses** A decorative and protective treatment for new and old bare timber surfaces (both softwood and hardwood) in interior and exterior locations. Ideal for timber cladding, window frames, doors, fences and sheds. Not suitable for use on painted or varnished timber
	Special properties Very easy to apply, protects timber from rot and attack from other wood-destroying organisms, resists blistering and peeling, a fresh coat does not require removal of the old coat
	Colour range A variety of wood tones
	Pack sizes 750 ml, 2.5 litres and 5 litres
	Spreading rate Approximately 15 square metres per litre, depending on the porosity of the timber
	Drying time Under normal conditions, touch-dry in two to four hours; can be recoated after 16 to 24 hours
	Equipment cleaner White spirit or turpentine substitute
	Storage Replace lid firmly; store away from heat and flame
	Surface preparation Ensure timber is sound, clean and dry (the moisture content should be less than 20%). Old paint or varnish should be stripped off and grey, weathered timber should be sanded until clean and bright. Bare softwood should be treated with a preservative and then allowed to dry. Some hardwoods, such as teak, have a naturally occurring oiliness which must be cleaned off with white spirit and the surface left to dry.
	Application Apply two coats of protective wood stain with a brush, allowing overnight drying between coats.

High-build wood stain *A highly durable, microporous, translucent, semi-gloss finish; air-drying and solvent-based*	**Uses** The flexible, microporous properties of high-build wood stain make it particularly suitable for the protection and decoration of exterior timber surfaces. Ideal for window frames, sills, doors, cladding and other high-grade exterior wooden surfaces **Special properties** Highly flexible film withstands normal changes in timber without cracking or loss of adhesion, reduced risk of blistering and flaking **Colour range** A variety of wood tones **Pack sizes** 750 ml, 2.5 litres and 5 litres **Spreading rate** Approximately 15 square metres per litre, depending on the porosity of the timber **Drying time** Under normal conditions, touch-dry in four to six hours; can be recoated after 24 hours **Equipment cleaner** White spirit or turpentine substitute **Storage** Replace lid firmly; store away from heat and flame **Surface preparation** Same as for protective wood stain **Application** Same as for protective wood stain

Table 8.4 Sealers and preparatory coatings

Knotting solution	**Uses** Applied to knots, resin patches and stains on timber surfaces, knotting solution seals timber ready for paint or varnish application
Generally formed from a solution of shellac (the resin of the Lac insect) and methylated spirits; air-drying and solvent-based	**Special properties** Fast-drying due to the methylated spirit content, suitable for use beneath a wide range of coatings including alkyds, chlorinated rubber and acrylics (but not alcohol-based coatings), available as aluminium-pigmented or titanium-pigmented varieties for use on smoke- and water-damaged surfaces
	Colour range Clear (unless pigmented variety)
	Pack sizes 250 ml to 1 litre
	Spreading rate Approximately 10 square metres per litre
	Drying time Under normal conditions, touch-dry in five to ten minutes; can be recoated after 30 minutes
	Equipment cleaner Mineralised methylated spirit
	Storage Replace lid firmly; store away from heat and flame
	Surface preparation Ensure that the surface is sound, clean and dry. Rub down surface with abrasive paper in order to provide a good key
	Application Shake tin well before use. Apply a full coat with the minimum of brush work. If a second coat is required it can be applied after 30 minutes, but brushing must be kept to a minimum in order to avoid any working-up of the underlying film.

Universal preservative	**Uses** Can be applied to new softwood that has not yet been treated with a preservative. Also suited as a pre-treatment coating for weathered timber surfaces, providing that the underlying wood is still sound
A clear fluid made from a blend of fungicide and alkyd resins mixed in a penetrative mineral solvent; air-drying and solvent-based	**Special properties** Contains fungicide
	Colour range Clear
	Pack sizes 1 litre, 2.5 litres and 5 litres
	Spreading rate Approximately 10 to 12 square metres per litre, depending on the porosity of the timber
	Drying time Under normal conditions, approximately 16 to 24 hours
	Equipment cleaner White spirit or turpentine
	Storage Replace lid firmly; store away from heat and flame
	Surface preparation Ensure that the surface is sound, clean and dry
	Application Stir well before use and apply one generous coat with a brush, paying particular attention to the end grain and joints. If any drill holes or cuts are present in the timber, re-treat them with the preservative after drying
Red oxide primer	**Uses** For priming iron and steel surfaces
An anti-corrosive priming paint for metal surfaces made from zinc phosphate and red oxide pigments in an alkyd medium; air-drying and solvent-based	**Special properties** Contains no added lead or chromate pigments, provides excellent adhesion
	Colour range Red
	Pack sizes 2.5 litres and 5 litres
	Spreading rate Approximately 11 square metres per litre, depending on the surface to be treated
	Drying time Under normal conditions, touch-dry in four to six hours; hard-dry and can be recoated after 16 to 24 hours

	Equipment cleaner White spirit or turpentine substitute
	Storage Replace lid firmly; store away from heat and flame
	Surface preparation Ensure surface is sound, clean and dry. Remove rust or millscale and any loose or defective paint, stripping to the bare surface if necessary
	Application Stir thoroughly before use. To ensure the best results, the brush should be fully loaded. Do not thin

chapter 9

Applying paint and creating special effects

OVERVIEW

Paint can be applied to a surface in a variety of different ways. Each method of paint application has its advantages and disadvantages and should be chosen according to the type of surface, the type of paint and the finished effect that is desired.

The way paint is applied to a surface can also produce some interesting and decorative finishes. Special effects such as texture, pattern and the illusion of a different surface can all be created by a skilled decorator and the contents of their toolbox.

Applying gold leaf to a surface, in a process known as gilding, can produce a very dramatic finish and is another type of special effect you may be asked to create.

In this chapter you will learn about:

- Getting started
- Applying paint using various pieces of equipment
- Creating special effects with paint
- Gilding.

Getting started

Opening a tin of paint and decanting

You may think that there is not much to opening a tin of paint and **decanting** it into a work pot. However, if you follow a few golden rules at the very beginning of a painting job, you will find that the rest of the job is much easier.

- It is always best to work from a work pot and not the stock pot. This is because a full stock pot will be heavy and difficult to manage. In addition, if a stock pot is knocked over, you will lose a lot of paint.

- Gently dust the stock pot before you open it. This will greatly reduce the amount of dust and debris that gets into the paint.

- Most paints require a thorough stir before use, but always check the manufacturer's instructions first, just in case they advise different treatment of the paint.

- Decant paint *slowly* from the back of the stock pot into a work pot. By pouring from the back of the tin, the front is kept clean, which will help it to be quickly identified when it is on a shelf.

- Only pour enough paint into the work pot to work from (usually to the height of the bristles on a paint brush).

- Keep a paint brush or cloth handy when decanting the paint, ready to wipe up any spills from the stock pot.

Remember the golden rules when decanting paint

Applying paint using various pieces of equipment

Brush application

Applying paint with a brush is not as popular as it used to be and is now often replaced with roller application. In order to achieve a high-quality finish with brush application, the following three actions should be followed:

1. Working in the brush and getting a dip.

2. Cutting in.

3. Laying off.

Working in the brush and getting a dip

Working in the brush means dipping the brush into the paint and then gently rubbing the brush against the inside of the work pot until all the bristles are evenly coated with paint. If you were to simply dip the brush into the paint and then start painting, you would only have paint on the outer bristles of the brush. After you have worked in the brush, you can scrape the brush against the top of the work pot in order to get it back into shape.

Remember

Make sure your work area is properly protected before starting any paint job. Putting up 'wet paint' signs is a very good idea

Working in a brush ensures that all of the bristles are coated with paint

Getting a dip means applying paint to the brush, ready to begin painting. Get a dip by dipping the brush into the paint and then tapping alternate sides of the brush on to a dry area of the inside of the work pot. This action locks the paint into the bristles, stopping it from dripping or spilling during the transfer from work pot to surface.

Remember

Don't scrape the brush on the edge of the work pot to remove excess paint. The only time you should do this is when you need to empty the brush of paint, for example, when preparing to wash it out

Getting a dip will ensure that paint stays on the brush until you apply it to the surface

Cutting in gives a clean and straight line

Cutting in

Cutting in is the action of applying paint to one surface while keeping paint off an adjoining surface; for example, when painting a wall, keeping paint off the ceiling, or when painting the putty in a window, keeping paint off the glass.

Cutting in is normally done first so that the paint is applied in sections small enough to handle (i.e. just enough to keep the edge of the applied paint wet). A dip of paint can then be applied in a vertical (up and down) motion. The paint can then be crossed, which means moving the paint in a sideways motion with the brush in order to spread it evenly.

Laying off

Laying off is done at the end of the paint application process and prevents misses and runs and ensures the paint is evenly spread. It is an action that the painter must perform in order to achieve the best possible finish. As the brush is brought down the surface, a small 'roll' of paint forms in front of the bristles. If the brush is not lifted off the surface by moving it back in the opposite direction, a run or sag will form. Figures 9.1 to 9.3 show the procedure for laying off.

Did you know?

You should apply paint in a methodical manner. If painting a wall, start at the top and cut into any dissimilar surfaces first

Remember

Laying off will need lots of practice to perfect

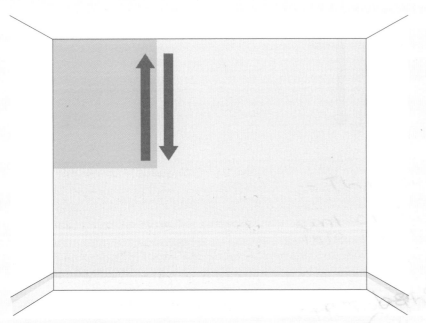

Figure 9.1 Step 1 Move the brush in a vertical motion (up and down)

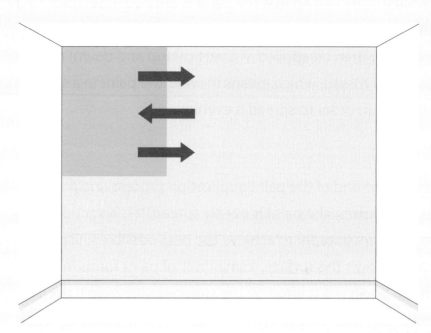

Figure 9.2 Step 2 Move the brush in a horizontal motion (side to side)

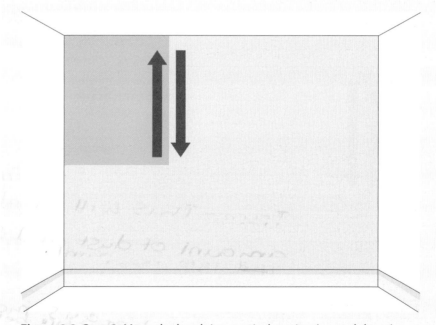

Figure 9.3 Step 3 Move the brush in a vertical motion (up and down)

Laying off emulsion paint requires a slightly different brush movement. The brush should be moved across the surface in an arcing motion so that it doesn't run or sag.

Roller application

Rollers come in various shapes and sizes to suit different surfaces and requirements. Table 9.1 shows examples of different roller types available, along with their purpose.

Laying off emulsion paint should be done with an arcing motion

Table 9.1 Roller types and their purposes

Roller type	Purpose
Large	Covering large surface areas
Small	Covering small surface areas
Curved	Covering curved or rounded surfaces, such as pipes
Small and thin with a long handle	Covering surfaces behind radiators and other difficult to reach areas
Long pile	Creating rough, textured paint finishes
Short pile	Creating smooth, untextured paint finishes

Whichever type of roller you use, you will need a container in which to hold the paint. A roller tray or a scuttle has a deep end that holds the paint, whilst a shallow rough area of the container is used to work the roller against in preparation for application to the surface.

The roller should be dipped into the paint and then repeatedly rolled against the rough part of the container. The rolling action removes excess paint from the roller, ensuring that the right amount of paint is applied to the surface. When painting a surface using a roller, use a 'W' motion. Laying off with a roller should be done in a vertical movement, which, if done well, will ensure that no lines are left on the surface.

Apply paint with a roller using a 'W' motion

Paint pad application

Paint pads have a short pile, usually mohair, attached to a cushion of foam. Paint pads can be used to apply all types of paint, whether water-based or oil-based. There are lots of different sizes available for different types of job, even pads small enough to cut in a sash window. The paint pad head is usually removable for easy cleaning.

Remember

Paint pads should only be cleaned using water or white spirit. Stronger solvents and other types of brush cleaner may attack the sponge

Paint pads are available in a variety of sizes and shapes

Paint mitten application

As the name suggests, paint mittens are worn on the hand. The palm-side of the mitten is covered in sheepskin and is the part of the mitten used to apply the paint. Mitten application of paint is not the most accurate method, however, it can be effective when painting around pipes and railings.

Definition

Atomised – when a liquid is broken up into tiny droplets like a mist

Spray application

When paint is applied to a surface with a sprayer, the stream of paint that flows from the nozzle is broken up and **atomised**. The main advantage of this method of application is that a relatively smooth film of paint can be applied very quickly.

The process of spray painting is very complex and is normally undertaken only by specialists. However, any decorator may get the occasional job when a spray finish is required, such as multi-colour finishes or metallic paint finishes on radiators.

A paint sprayer is ideal for large jobs

Dipping

Dipping involves immersing an object in a container of paint and then lifting it out to dry. This technique is mainly used in an industrial setting because it is a quick method of coating intricate surfaces in paint, ensuring that all nooks and crannies are fully covered, even the inside of tubes and pipes. Dipping results in little paint waste as any excess paint drops back into the container.

Creating special effects with paint

In this section, we will look at some of the many special paint effects that can be created by a decorator. Table 9.2 briefly details the surface preparation that will be required to create certain special effects.

Safety tip

Make sure you are wearing the correct PPE when producing special effects

Table 9.2 Surface preparation for special paint effects

Special effect	Preparation required
Broken colours (effects that produce a multi-coloured finish)	• A clean and hard surface with no brush marks, indents or nibs • Good quality undercoat such as oil-based eggshell
Graining	• An oil- and grease-free surface • The surface should be rubbed down between coats to provide a good key • To provide the background colour for the grain effect, an eggshell paint (normally oil-based) should be applied first and stippled to remove brush marks. A second coat should be applied in the same manner and left to dry thoroughly
Marbling	• Same as preparation for graining • The correct choice of background colour and the type of marbling to be imitated are essential parts of the effect

Preparation for graining involves creating a clean, brush mark-free surface with a good key

Find out

Why might a client desire a graining effect on a surface?

Definition

Scumble – a semi-transparent coating containing pigment and linseed oil

Graining

Imitating wood grain on non-timber surfaces has been carried out for centuries. Creating this type of special effect requires a high level of skill, as well as some artistic ability. We will now look at how an imitation mahogany finish can be achieved, although the basic principles are similar for other types of wood graining.

Graining procedure

- Apply mahogany **scumble** to the ground coat (it should be a deep red).

- Apply the graining colour in one direction, creating a straight grain.

- Using a flogger and beating from bottom to top, work up the grain. The flogger simulates the pore marks in wood.

- Apply some Van Dyke brown with a touch of black colouring.

- Using a mottler, dip into the mixed Van Dyke brown and, using a half scrub with a sideways motion, move it down the length of work to be grained. This will give the impression of dark and light streaks.

- Soften the work with a badger softener.

- Finally, use a smaller mottler to distress the darker markings by half dragging and dabbing in short strokes down the wall.

- The straight grain marks you have just applied should be almost at right angles to the heavier streaks. When the graining effect is dry, the surface must be varnished to enhance and protect the effect.

Applying scumble to surface

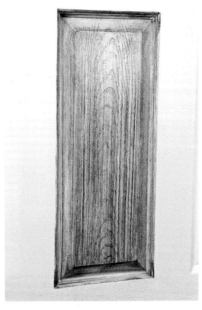

The finished graining effect

Dragging and combing

Dragging and combing are decorative effects usually associated with graining, but they are created with paint colours and glazes, rather than graining colours. When used with broken colour, dragging and combing produces a stylised version of the grain effect. An oil-based ground coat colour is best.

A comb can be used to create a simple paint effect, as shown here, or more intricate patterns with practice

It is possible to produce many patterns by dragging and combing, including a straight timber grain, raw silk and even woven cotton combing effects.

Step 1 Apply the glaze sparingly to the surface, laying off vertically

Step 2 Drag a brush through the glaze to create uneven lines. The ground coat should show through just enough to create a two-tone effect

Step 3 The finished dragging paint effect

Marbling

Many decorators will use a standard technique when creating this special effect, while others with a more artistic flare will create their own original designs for each job. The following procedure describes how to create a marble effect called 'vert de mer', which is a black and green marble originating from Northern Italy. Vert de mer marbling is a pleasing yet dramatic marble with a variety of interesting features.

Find out

What does 'vert de mer' mean?

Did you know?

Marble is rock that has been exposed to extreme temperatures and high pressures within the Earth. The end result is a hard substance, normally with a coloured swirl or clouded appearance, which can take a high polish

Step 1 Apply an oil-based black eggshell ground coat, ensuring an indentation- and brush mark-free finish

Definition

Driers – a liquid chemical that promotes drying

Step 2 When the ground coat is dry, apply a thin layer of glip (two parts turpentine to one part linseed oil, adding 10% **driers** to finish the mixture)

Step 3 Apply dark green paint to the ground coat and allow to dry

Step 4 Apply pale green paint to the surface and allow to dry

Step 5 Stipple with a hog hair stippler. This will blend the two shades of green, losing the sharp edges of the colours

Step 6 Distress the surface with a plastic bag, exposing the ground colour

Step 7 Apply white spirit to the surface by flicking it onto the surface from a paint brush. This will open up the colours

Step 8 Mix a white eggshell paint and create fine lines on the surface using a feather or sable writer. This is done by dipping the tip of the feather in the paint and then slowly dragging it across the surface, twisting it as you drag

Step 9 Soften the white lines using a dry brush. Protect the paint effect with a layer of varnish

Rag rolling

Rag rolling is a broken colour effect created by applying colour to a surface with a rag and then lifting the colour off with the rag, exposing some of the background colour. 'Ragging on' is the name given to the action of applying the colour to a ground coat. 'Ragging off' is the name given to the action of lifting off some of the colour and creates a different effect. The rag used should be **lint**-free and bunched up in the hand during paint application. A chamois leather roller (Duet® type) or even rolled up paper or plastic bags can be used instead of a rag and will create a softer or sharper effect.

Rag rolling procedure

- Apply a coloured glaze to the surface, removing any brush marks with a hog hair stippler.

- Bunch up a rag and dip it into the paint, making sure that it is completely saturated. Wring out the rag and then roll it into a loose cylinder and twist it slightly. You can now apply the paint by rolling the rag across small sections of the surface.

- Apply or lift off the colour randomly using either another rag or a paper or plastic bag.

A rag rolling paint effect can be more interesting than solid colour

Sponging

Sponging is quite simply creating a broken colour effect by applying and removing paint with a sponge. Either a natural or synthetic sponge can be used.

Sponging procedure

- Apply a coloured eggshell or thinned gloss paint and allow to dry completely.

- Decant the paint to be sponged into a tray. Load the sponge with colour by dipping it into the paint and squeezing out excess paint.

- Apply the colour to the base coat by gently dabbing with the sponge, ensuring you don't overload areas with paint.

- If desired, build up different layers of colour with the sponge, allowing each coat to dry thoroughly. Different types of sponge could also be used for each colour, giving the finished paint effect the appearance of depth and texture.

Did you know?

A natural sponge is the soft and fibrous skeleton of a marine animal

Sponging is an easy way to create an interesting broken colour effect

Stippling

Stippling is a way of creating a soft, suede-like appearance on a surface. Different colours can also be overlayed in order to create bands of colour. Water-based paints allow the decorator to apply a number of colours in one day, however, the colour must be applied swiftly as the drying process will be rapid.

Stippling procedure

Step 1 Mix up a glaze consisting of colour turpentine and driers. Apply the glaze to the surface with a brush

Step 2 Use a hog hair stippler to stipple the glaze, ensuring no brush marks remain. The aim is to achieve a soft, even texture

Wiping and glazing

Wiping and glazing is a highlighting technique used on **relief surfaces**. A relief surface is one that has parts that are raised or projecting out from the background. Embossed wallpaper, ornate panels and mouldings are all examples of relief surfaces.

Wiping and glazing procedure

- Apply a base coat to the surface and allow to dry.

- Apply a tinted glaze and stipple with a normal 3" brush to create an even blend with no light or dark patches.

- Immediately take a cloth or squeegee and wipe over the surface. The aim is to only remove the glaze from raised parts of the surface, leaving a two-tone effect.

Remember

Dispose of soiled cloths in a way that complies with COSHH regulations

Wipe over the surface with a cloth to create a two-tone paint effect

Stencilling

Stencilling is a way of decorating a surface with a pattern or design using a cut-out template. A client may ask for stencil work because:

- it produces a unique paint effect on a surface. The position and colour of the pattern or design will be unique and tailored to the client's requirements

- it is quick and easy to repeat a pattern or design

There are two kinds of stencil:

1. Positive stencils – where a pattern is cut out and paint is applied over the openings, reproducing the pattern on the surface beneath (see photo).

2. Negative stencils – the opposite of a positive stencil, whereby the background of a pattern is cut out.

A positive stencil

Stencils can be made up of more than one part. These are known as multi-plate stencils. For example, a stencil of a flower design may be made up of three plates: the first for the leaves and stem, the second for the first layer of petals and the third for the top layer of petals and flower centre. Multi-plate stencils are particularly useful when a pattern is made up of lots of colours or when it is very complex. When using multi-plate stencils, ensure that you match up the plates or your finished design will not look as it should. Lining up the plates with two pencil lines at right angles is the most effective method.

Stencilling procedure

- Mix up enough colour to create the stencil and have a stencil brush and palette for each colour.

- Put a small amount of colour onto each palette. You may want to tape up the ends of your brushes to stop the ends splaying.

- Load up a brush with the first colour and stipple it on a clean area of the palette until the colour is even.

- Apply the colour to the stencil, holding the brush at a right angle to the surface.

- Allow each colour to dry thoroughly before applying the next.

Remember

When creating your own stencils, seal the card with knotting solution to prevent them from becoming soggy. Be careful when using a craft knife and never cut towards the hand holding the stencil. When cutting out curves, move the material you are cutting rather than the knife

Gilding

Gilding is the application of gold or other metal leaf to a surface. The procedure has to be carried out with great care, both in terms of working practice and preparation of the surface.

A gilded surface

Did you know?

23 carat and 24 carat gold leaf will not tarnish and does not need a protective coating

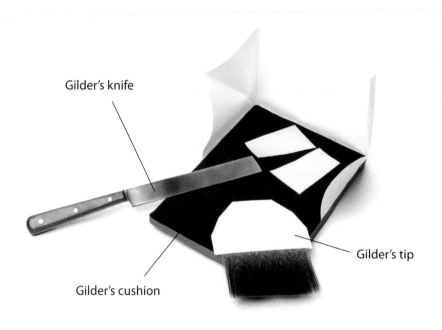

Gilder's knife

Gilder's tip

Gilder's cushion

Loose leaf may be applied from a gilder's cushion

There are two types of gilding:

1. transfer leaf is when the leaf comes attached to a thin piece of tissue paper and is applied to a surface in the same way you would apply a transfer.

2. loose leaf is a more skilled operation as the leaf is loose and applied either from a book of gold leaf or from a gilder's cushion.

Surface preparation

In order to ensure gold leaf only adheres to the parts of the surface you want it to adhere to, one of the following should be applied prior to gilding:

- egg glair – the white of an egg is added to a litre of warm water and the mixture shaken to produce froth. The glair is then applied to the surface, followed by application of gold size (see page 215 for more information on gold size). When the surface reaches the right level of tackiness, the gold leaf can be applied. Finally, the surface should be washed down with clean, warm water to remove all of the glair and any gold leaf that has not adhered.

- French chalk – is a soft white chalk and is used in a similar way to egg glair.

Did you know?

The block of chalk in a bicycle puncture repair kit is compressed French chalk

Gold size

Gold size is an adhesive substance used as a **mordant** for gold leaf application. After applying gold size to a surface it must be left for a suitable length of time to reach the right level of tack (stickiness).

Gold size is available in two forms: oil gold size and Japan gold size. Table 9.3 gives some more details about each type.

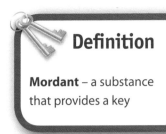

Definition

Mordant – a substance that provides a key

Table 9.3 Oil and Japan gold size

Gold size type	Uses	Drying time	Notes
Oil gold size	Suited to large metal or wooden surfaces. Not suitable for use with leaf other than gold	24 to 30 hours	Needs to be well brushed out to ensure no runs or snags. Ensure no dust settles on the surface
Japan gold size	Suited to lettering and ornamental work	Available with a ½-, 1-, 2-, 4-, and 8- hour drying time	Use Japan size when weather or dust is likely to affect surface

Transfer leaf application procedure

- Prepare the surface as described above and apply gold size.

- Wait until the surface has the right amount of tack and then begin to apply the transfer leaf. The leaf will be attached to a piece of waxed paper.

- Gently rub the waxed paper with some cotton wool, thus transferring the leaf onto the size. See Figure 9.4.

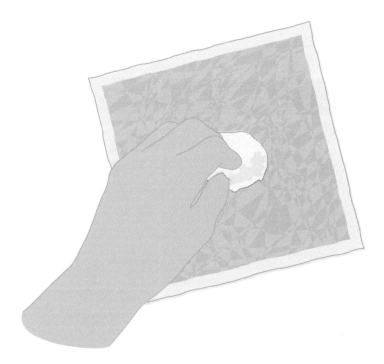

Gently rubbing the wax paper with cotton wool transfers the gold leaf to the surface

Figure 9.4 Applying transfer leaf to a surface

Loose leaf application procedure

- Prepare the surface as described above and apply gold size.

- Wait until the surface has the right amount of tack and then begin to apply the loose leaf. The leaf can only be handled with a gilder's tip and cushion and the procedure will take time to perfect. In order to pick up the leaf, static or grease has to applied to the gilder's tip. The easiest way of achieving this is by rubbing the tip on your forehead. The tip can then be held to the cushion, whereby the loose leaf attaches to the tip.

- Gently brush off any excess gold leaf that has not adhered to the surface with a cotton wool pad.

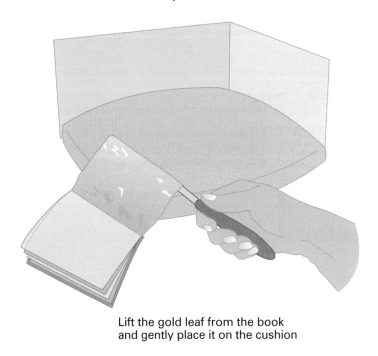

Lift the gold leaf from the book
and gently place it on the cushion

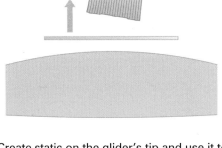

Create static on the glider's tip and use it to
pick up the leaf for application to the surface

Figure 9.5 Applying loose leaf to a surface

When applying either transfer leaf or loose leaf that is not 23 carat or 24 carat gold, it will need to be protected with a layer of **rabbit skin size** followed by a layer of suitable varnish or lacquer. Leaf that is 23 or 24 carat gold will also benefit from a protective layer, shielding it from wear and tear.

Definition

Rabbit skin size
– a substance made from animal tissues, which is applied before a layer of varnish, as varnish alone will discolour the gold

Gilding defects

As you have already read, gilding needs lots of practice. During your training, you may discover some of the problems that can occur when gilding. Figure 9.6 details some of the gilding defects that can occur, along with their causes.

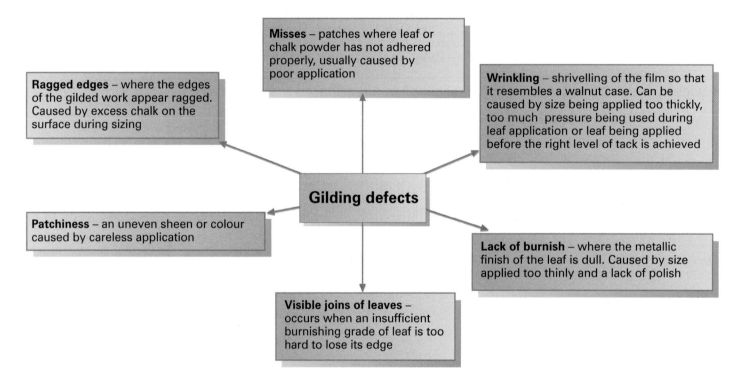

Misses – patches where leaf or chalk powder has not adhered properly, usually caused by poor application

Wrinkling – shrivelling of the film so that it resembles a walnut case. Can be caused by size being applied too thickly, too much pressure being used during leaf application or leaf being applied before the right level of tack is achieved

Ragged edges – where the edges of the gilded work appear ragged. Caused by excess chalk on the surface during sizing

Patchiness – an uneven sheen or colour caused by careless application

Gilding defects

Lack of burnish – where the metallic finish of the leaf is dull. Caused by size applied too thinly and a lack of polish

Visible joins of leaves – occurs when an insufficient burnishing grade of leaf is too hard to lose its edge

Figure 9.6 Gilding defects

FAQ

What does the term 'broken colour' mean?

A 'broken colour' paint effect is one that is created by layering paint colours and then breaking them up to reveal the underlying colours. This can be achieved by adding colour (for example, when sponging) or by taking off colour (for example, when ragging off). A broken colour paint effect can give a surface the appearance of shading and texture.

On the job: The paint sprayer

Rob is working on a new build site. He is a first-year apprentice and is proving to be a very quick learner. Rob's boss comes and tells him that when he has finished what he is doing, Rob is to go and get a paint sprayer and start a new job using this piece of equipment. Rob tells his boss that he has never used a paint sprayer before. Rob's boss says that the instructions are in the box and Rob should be able to work it out.

What do you think Rob should do? Do you think Rob's boss is right to ask Rob to carry out this task?

Knowledge check

1. Why is it best to work from a work pot instead of a stock pot?

2. What is 'getting a dip' and what does this action do?

3. Briefly describe laying off.

4. If applying paint with a roller, what could you use to hold the paint?

5. When might a mitten be a good way of applying paint?

6. What is a broken colour effect?

7. What types of pattern can be achieved with dragging and combing?

8. Name two types of material that could be used instead of a rag to lift off colour during rag rolling.

9. What is a relief surface?

10. Name two types of stencil and describe how they differ.

11. What is egg glair and how would it be used?

12. How might wrinkling of gold leaf be caused?

chapter 10

Applying surface coverings

OVERVIEW

One way to change the look of a room is to apply a surface covering – wallpaper. The earliest example of wallpaper dates to around 1500. These papers were hand-painted and nailed on to timber, which was then fixed on to walls. Printed wallpaper on rolls first became available in 1841. Nowadays, there is a huge range of wall coverings to choose from – from basic woodpulp wallpapers to fabric wall coverings. A decorator may be asked to hang wallpaper on ceilings as well as walls in both domestic and commercial premises.

This chapter will cover:

- Preparing surfaces for papering

- Working out wallpaper quantities

- Wallpaper adhesives and papering equipment

- Preparing to apply surface coverings

- Application of surface coverings

- Types of surface covering

- Surface covering defects.

Preparing surfaces for papering

The following general good practice should be followed when preparing a surface for wallpapering:

- ensure the surface is sound, clean, dry and free from grease. Wallpaper will not stick to grease and dirt and it is also unhygienic to paper over dirty surfaces

- surfaces must be in good condition. Flaking paint should be rubbed down with medium abrasive sandpaper back to a firm surface, then sealed and filled. Powdery or crumbling surfaces should be painted with stabilising solution or PVA resin

- gloss or eggshell surfaces should be roughened with abrasive paper to provide a good key for the wallpaper paste

- prepared gloss surfaces can be covered with PVA adhesive to improve sticking

- any nail or screw heads must be primed with a metal primer to prevent rust staining.

We will now look at the preparation of some specific surfaces.

Painted surfaces

Preparing previously painted surfaces for wallpaper is very similar to the preparation required before applying paint. For further information, see Chapter 7 Preparation of surfaces page 135.

Bare plaster surfaces

Definition

Sized – sealed

Bare plaster surfaces should be **sized** with a purpose-made size or wallpaper adhesive or paste, such as cellulose paste or tub paste. Do not use starch paste to size plaster as this will flake when it dries, leaving an unsound surface.

Sizing is essential as it evens out the **porosity** of the bare plaster and prevents the water within wallpaper paste from being absorbed by the plaster. When this happens, known as 'snatch', the decorator will be unable to slide the wallpaper into position.

Some products, such as universal wall covering primer, are designed to allow the easy stripping of wallpaper when the room is next decorated. A thick coat of emulsion can also be used to size bare plaster.

Sizing will prevent plaster absorbing water from paste

New plaster must be allowed to dry out. Hard wall plaster may need up to six months to dry thoroughly before it is ready for wallpapering. Plasterboard that has been coated with board finish plaster (or scim) can be papered as soon as the plaster is visibly dry.

Plasterboard surfaces

If new plasterboard has been sized with a suitable adhesive or emulsion, the wallpaper will bond to the surface. However, removing the wallpaper at a later date could leave the paper surface of the plasterboard stripped or badly damaged (see Chapter 7 page 153). To avoid this, the surface should be sized with an oil-based primer, which will make the paper surface of the plasterboard waterproof and less likely to damage when paper is stripped from it. Alternatively, a wall covering primer can be used.

If removing wallpaper from the surface, all traces of old paste and small pieces of wallpaper should be removed by using water and a paste brush and scrubbing the surface. A Scotch-Brite® pad can also be used to do this. Finally, use a sponge and some clean water to rinse off the surface.

Definition

Porosity – the ability of a surface to allow water through

Working out wallpaper quantities

There are two main methods of calculating how much wallpaper you will require:

Method 1 Use a roll of wallpaper as a width guide to measure the number of full lengths required. Mark where the joints will appear along the wall or ceiling. Then measure the length of the ceiling or height of the wall to discover how many full lengths can be cut from one roll.

Method 2 Measure up a room or take dimensions from a drawing. Calculate the total surface area of the room, including windows and doors. Then work out the area of the offtakes (things that will not be papered, such as the doors and windows) and subtract this amount from the total surface area. This will give you the surface area that requires papering. Next, find out the surface area of a roll of wallpaper and divide it into the surface area. This will give you an idea of how many rolls of wallpaper you will need.

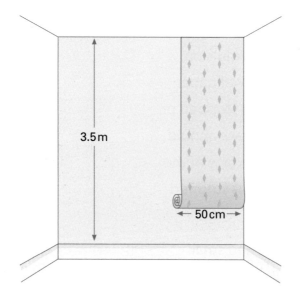

Method 1 – use the width of a roll of wallpaper and measure the height of the wall

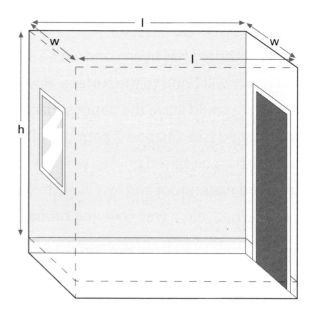

Method 2 – calculate the total surface area of the room and then subtract the offtakes (e.g. doors and windows)

Figure 10.1 Working out wallpaper quantities

To ensure you get the right quantity of wallpaper, you will need to allow for wastage. This is usually 15–20 per cent depending on the type of pattern, shape and height of the room. To be on the safe side, a decorator should work on 20 per cent wastage.

Wallpaper adhesives and papering equipment

There are three main types of wallpaper adhesive. They each have a different moisture content (low, medium and high) and you will need to choose the right one for the job.

Adhesives are available in:

- ready-mixed tubs, in heavy-, medium- or light-grades
- sachets or boxes of powder which require water to be added

Adhesives are also available for use with very specific wall coverings.

Did you know?

Most modern adhesives contain a fungicide to prevent mould growth

Ready-mixed adhesive

Ready-mixed tub adhesives have a very low moisture content. They contain a chemical called PVA, which improves the adhesive property of the paste (how well it sticks). Some tub adhesives are very thick and must be diluted before use.

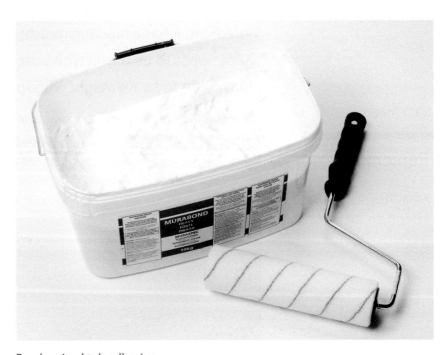

Ready mixed tub adhesive

Table 10.1 Advantages and disadvantages of tub adhesive

Advantages	Disadvantages
Very good adhesive properties. Ideal for use with vinyl and contract vinyl such as Muraspec®	Expensive
Can be used to size surfaces	
Can be applied directly to wall surfaces to hang certain types of wall covering	
Contains a fungicide to prevent mould growth	
Does not rot and remains useable for a long time	

Adhesives that are mixed with water

Starch adhesive

Starch adhesive is also known as flour adhesive as wheat flour is its main ingredient. It has a medium moisture content and comes in powder form which needs to be mixed with water to produce a paste that is suitable for lightweight to heavyweight woodpulp wallpapers.

Table 10.2 Advantages and disadvantages of starch adhesive

Advantages	Disadvantages
Good adhesive properties. Suitable for hanging heavy textured preparatory papers	More expensive than cellulose adhesive
Contains a fungicide so can be used with vinyl papers	May stain the face of the wallpaper
	Difficult to mix
	Adhesive will rot and so is only useable for one to two days

Cellulose adhesive

Cellulose adhesive has the highest water content of any paste and comes in powder form which needs to be mixed with cold water before use. It is used with lightweight wallpapers such as lining papers and vinyls.

Table 10.3 Advantages and disadvantages of cellulose adhesive

Advantages	Disadvantages
Inexpensive	Less adhesive than starch paste
Little risk of staining	Can cause paper to over-expand, resulting in wrinkling or mismatch
Easy to apply	If used on wallpaper that is unable to let water pass through it, such as vinyl, the water content in the adhesive may be prevented from drying out through the paper, leading to damage
Easy to mix	
Does not rot and can remain useable for a long time	
Contains a fungicide to prevent mould growth	

Adhesives designed for specific wall coverings

- Border adhesive is ideal for applying vinyl on vinyl, for example when applying a border paper on top of another paper. It has strong adhesive properties.

- Lincrusta glue is a very strong adhesive with good bonding properties.

- Overlap adhesive is designed for bonding vinyl to vinyl. It can be used on vinyl to bond overlaps on internal/external angles and to apply border paper over vinyl.

Equipment

Table 10.4 Wallpapering equipment

Equipment	Description	Dos and don'ts
Paste brush	A 175 mm flat brush makes a good paste brush	Choose a brush with synthetic bristles as these are not affected by mildew and can be left in paste for long periods of time
Pasteboard	Used for pasting wallpaper, arranging paper and for splitting lengths of paper	Keep clean and free from paste at all times as a dirty pasteboard will lead to a poor-quality papering job
Paste bucket	Used for mixing paste	Clean out after use and before mixing paste. If the sides of the bucket are thick with old paste, when mixing fresh paste the new paste may become lumpy
Plumb bob	A weight attached to a piece of string. Used to mark a vertical line (the plumb line) on to walls before hanging paper	You must be accurate when using a plumb bob because the measurements it provides act as a starting point for papering and the first line marked will affect every following length of paper

Marking a plumb line

- Mark your plumb line only once it stops swinging.

- Make sure that the string is hanging freely – check it isn't snagged on anything.

- Use only one eye to sight the plumb line and continue to use the same eye for every mark you make.

A plumb bob must be used accurately

- When marking your pencil line against the string, do not overstretch but move your head to the pencil and keep your aiming eye level to the mark that you are about to make.

- If you need to move your hand down the string, make sure that it does not move by using alternate hands to position the string.

Preparing to apply surface coverings

Before hanging surface coverings, always read the manufacturer's instructions. These will contain all the information required to hang the wallpaper correctly, including soaking time, recommended paste and surface preparation required.

It is important to check the pattern and batch number of each roll of wallpaper before cutting any. If papers with different batch numbers are used on the same wall, you may be able to see a variation in colour. Once you have checked the batch numbers, the rolls of paper should be rolled out and the paper looked at in natural light as variations may still occur in some batches, known as shading. Look out for the international performance symbols shown in most wallpaper instructions which offer easy-to-understand information at a glance.

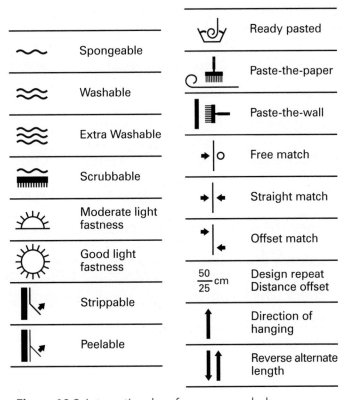

Spongeable	
Washable	
Extra Washable	
Scrubbable	
Moderate light fastness	
Good light fastness	
Strippable	
Peelable	
Ready pasted	
Paste-the-paper	
Paste-the-wall	
Free match	
Straight match	
Offset match	
Design repeat Distance offset	
Direction of hanging	
Reverse alternate length	

Figure 10.2 International performance symbols

Before paper hanging, set up your site by laying down a dustsheet, mixing the paste, erecting the pasteboard and finding a box to put all the waste cuttings in. All wall-mounted fixtures and fittings, such as blinds, curtain rails and wall lights, should be removed. Any exposed wires should be individually taped up with insulation tape to prevent electric shock.

Electrical fittings must be switched off at the mains and removed from the wall by a trained person. The screws should be relocated in their holes, which avoids the problem of finding the screw holes once the wall is covered with paper. Cross slits can then be cut in the paper to allow the screws and cables through. Once you have set up your work area, you can then think about how you are going to wallpaper the room.

Time spent planning is important, because a well set-up room can save a lot of time and effort and can help you to use paper more economically. For example, before starting you should work out how to avoid the length of paper you are hanging from conflicting with any straight edges such as doorframes, window frames and internal or external corners. Remember that some wallpapers are very expensive, and the decorator is responsible for getting the preparation right.

The following golden rules should always be followed when preparing to apply surface coverings:

- read the manufacturer's instructions supplied with each roll

- check each roll individually to ensure it is not damaged

- check that the batch numbers and shades are identical

- open the rolls to check the pattern and printing

- identify the pattern, for example **straight match** or **drop match** pattern

- check which way the paper should be applied. Some patterns are not easy to identify. If you are unsure, contact the client or the manufacturer.

Remember

Measure twice but only cut once. In other words, double-check your measurements before making the cut

Definition

Straight match – a wallpaper design that is repeated horizontally across the paper

Drop match – a wallpaper pattern that is not repeated horizontally across the paper

Application of surface coverings

If you have identified the wallpaper as a straight match, then lengths of paper can be cut from one roll at a time. If the pattern is a drop match, you should cut your lengths from two rolls. This is because two lengths of a drop match patterned paper cut to the same size from the same roll cannot be used adjacent to each other on a wall because they would not match.

To cut lengths from two rolls:

- Place two rolls on the pasteboard.

- Match the pattern at the edge using the two rolls.

- Trim both top edges so that the waste is equal.

- Label one roll A and the other B using a pencil on the back of each length. Keep on marking them alternately until all lengths are cut.

- Keep the lengths in order when pasting and hanging.

When the first length of wallpaper has been measured and cut from the roll, it can be used as a template for the cutting of the other required lengths. After offering the first cut length up to the wall, check that there have not been any measuring errors. If not, all of the full lengths can then be cut.

You are now ready to start pasting the lengths.

Remember

Keep the pasteboard free of paste at all times. Get into the habit of doing this every time you paste

Pasting procedure

1. Stand in front of the pasteboard and place the length of paper reverse side upwards.

2. Make a short overlap aligned with the furthest edge away from you.

3. Apply paste down the centre of the cut length.

4. Keep applying the paste from the centre to the furthest edge. Do not go from edge to centre because the paste will drop onto the face side of the paper.

5. Move the cut length to the nearest edge of the pasteboard and continue to work the paste brush from centre to edge, not from edge to centre.

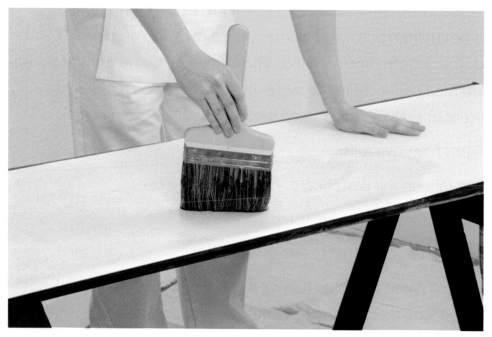

A good pasting technique

Definition

Equal stretch – supple and pliable to the same degree

Folding procedure

The paper should be allowed to soak before hanging, but to ensure **equal stretch** each length should have the same amount of soaking time. This can be done by working with two lengths at any one time, pasting one, then pasting the other before hanging the first length, and so on.

Now you are ready to fold a length of paper. How it is folded will depend on how long the length is or where it is to be hung.

Remember

For the correct amount of soaking time, follow the manufacturer's instructions. Check that the paper is pliable (bends easily) before you use it

*   Two-lap fold – if the wallpaper is of normal room length, you should use a two-lap fold, making the top fold the longest fold. It should be roughly two-thirds to one-third (see Figure 10.3).

*   Concertina fold – this series of small folds can be easily unfolded during the paper hanging process. The concertina fold is normally used for papering ceilings or for applying paper horizontally. It can also be used for folding very long lengths before vertical application.

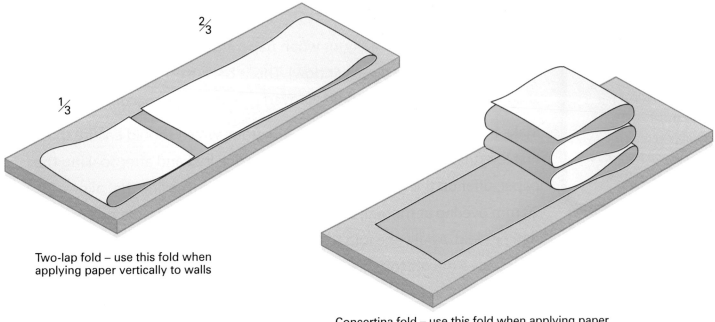

Two-lap fold – use this fold when applying paper vertically to walls

Figure 10.3 Types of wallpaper fold

Concertina fold – use this fold when applying paper horizontally to walls or when papering ceilings

Papering vertically

Take the first length of wallpaper and offer it up to the plumb line, with the longest fold opened and then place it on the wall. You should be able to slide the paper accurately towards the plumb line. Smooth the paper down with the brush, working from the centre towards the edges. When all the air is smoothed out, fold down the bottom fold and apply it to the wall as before.

Hanging paper vertically

Remember

Smooth out wallpaper from the centre to the edge. This pushes any air bubbles to the edge and out from the surface

Definition

Decorator's crutch – a rolled-up length of wallpaper or a piece of wood used to support a concertina fold

Papering horizontally

When papering horizontally, or when papering a ceiling, always work away from any light source (i.e. a window). This is because a light source will create shadows on the surface should an overlap in the paper occur.

Make a chalk line on the ceiling to work from, which should ensure that the first length is straight. Always use a concertina fold and after soaking the paper, offer up the first length to the ceiling against a line that allows for a 20 mm overlap at the wall edge. The concertina folds should be around 350 mm per fold. Apply one fold to the ceiling while supporting the unopened folds with a **decorator's crutch**. Smooth out the first fold. Then open one more fold and repeat the process – do not try to apply more than one fold at a time. When free of air pockets and creases, the paper should be trimmed out to both wall edges.

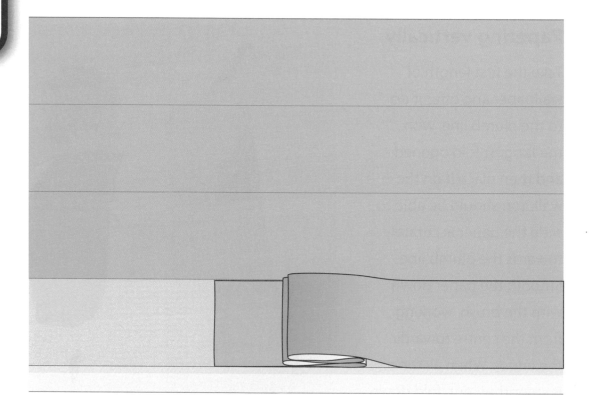

Figure 10.4 Papering horizontally

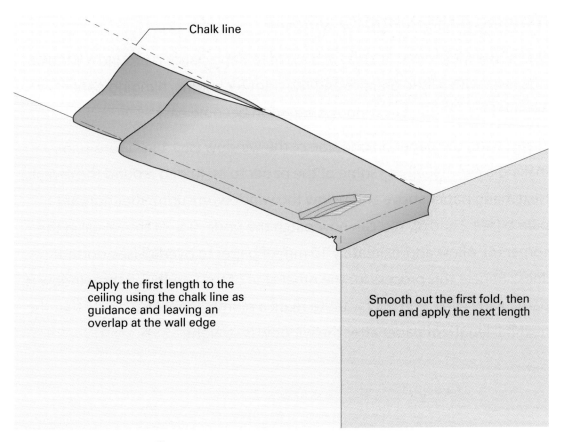

Chalk line

Apply the first length to the ceiling using the chalk line as guidance and leaving an overlap at the wall edge

Smooth out the first fold, then open and apply the next length

Figure 10.5 Papering a ceiling

Hanging paper around a window

One of the most difficult areas in a room to hang paper is around a window. However, with a little practise and the right technique, hanging paper around features such as windows will soon become easy.

Firstly, hang the paper on one side of the window (see 1 in Figure 10.6), making a cut that allows some of the paper to be folded around the reveal. Next, hang paper above and below the window, ensuring that they are plumb (see 2 and 3). You can now patch the underside of the reveal in the corner (4). Allow approximately 10 mm of paper to overlap (see dotted lines). Repeat this process for the other side of the window. If the window is particularly wide, you may want to mark a plumb line to make sure that the next full length of paper after the window is straight.

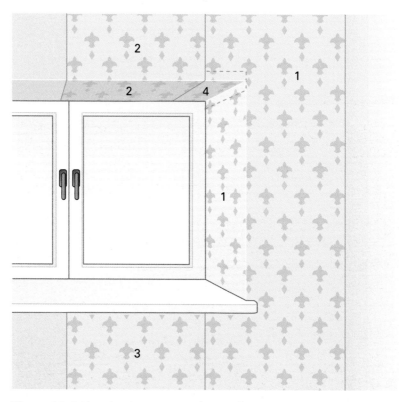

Figure 10.6 Hanging paper around a window

Paper hanging a staircase

When applying paper to a staircase always start with the longest drop (length). After applying this first length, work from either side of it.

Table 10.5 gives some general golden rules you should follow when folding and pasting a surface covering.

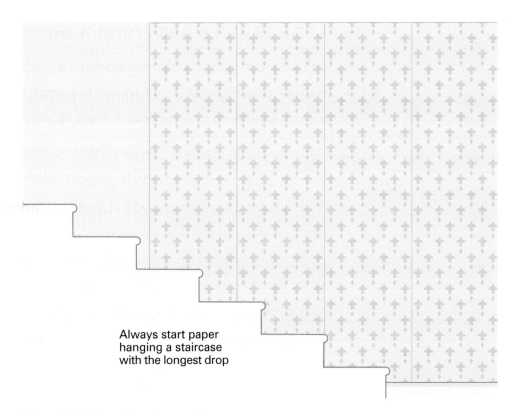

Always start paper hanging a staircase with the longest drop

Figure 10.7 Paper hanging a staircase

Table 10.5 Dos and don'ts when folding and pasting

Do	Don't
Remove lumps from the paste	Leave areas of the covering unpasted
Remove any loose bristles from pasted lengths	Get paste on the pasteboard or the face side of the paper
Leave the top and bottom 50 mm of the length dry so it may be handled	Mix paste too thinly
Keep edges parallel (aligned) when folding	Place the paste bucket on the pasteboard
Keep all tools and equipment clean	Have an untidy work area
Check that you are using the right paste for the paper and its application	

Centralising a patterned wallpaper

Figure 10.8 shows a chimney breast and alcoves of a room papered with a patterned wallpaper. The wallpaper has a set pattern and the pattern match is horizontally set – it does not drop. The wallpaper has been centralised – that means that the first length of wallpaper has been placed in the centre of the chimney breast. Notice how this creates a balanced effect.

Figure 10.8 Centralising patterned wallpaper on a chimney breast

The chimney breast is a **focal point** of a room and can be the place to start papering if the whole room is to be papered in the same patterned paper. If a room does not have a chimney breast, choose one wall of the room as the feature wall and start paper hanging from the centre of that wall to ensure that the pattern of the paper is centralised.

Back trimming

Back trimming, also known as double cutting, is a technique of cutting through two sheets of wallpaper to achieve a perfect joint. This method is used on one-metre wide vinyl to achieve a butt joint.

Types of surface covering

Basic wallpapers

Basic wallpapers are made from either:

* wood pulp

* vinyl.

Wood pulp papers

Wood pulp papers can be used as preparatory papers or finish papers.

Preparatory papers are usually painted with emulsion to provide a finish or they can be used as a base underneath finish papers. The different types of preparatory papers include:

* plain, coloured and reinforced lining paper

* wood chip

* Anaglypta®.

Lining paper

Anaglypta® paper

Definition

Embossed – decorated with designs that stand out from surface

Finish papers are available in a variety of patterns:

- standard
- washable
- **embossed**.

Standard patterned wood pulp paper

Vinyl wallpapers

There are three basic categories of vinyl paper:

- standard patterned vinyl
- sculptured vinyl
- blown vinyl, which can be either a patterned finish paper or a preparatory paper requiring painting.

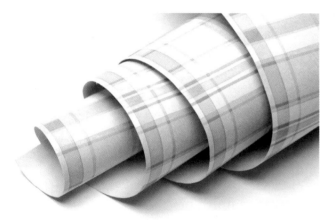

Standard patterned vinyl paper

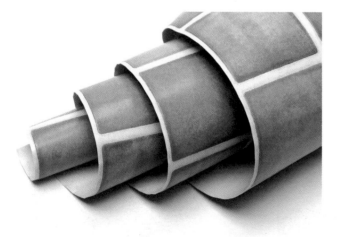

Sculptured vinyl paper

Patterned blown vinyl paper

Specialist surface coverings

Specialist coverings are those which are slightly different or unusual in some way from the standard papers already covered. They will probably only be used on particular jobs and in specific circumstances. Examples of specialist papers include:

- Cloth-backed vinyl – a paper that has a cotton backing and is textured to look like fabric. Usually used in high-traffic areas such as halls, corridors and public places.

- Lincrusta-Walton – a paper with a raised pattern or design that simulates carved plaster and wood. Usually used below dado rails, in pubs and restaurants and on staircases.

- Paper-backed Hessian – a fabric surface covering made from **jute**. Usually used as a decorative finish in offices and public buildings.

- Metal foil paper – a surface covering with a metal finish. Usually used as a very decorative covering on feature walls.

Definition

Jute – a rough fibre made from a tropical plant

Cloth-backed vinyl paper

Lincrusta-Walton

For further information on wallpaper types, see Tables 10.6 and 10.7 on pages 245 and 247.

Paper-backed Hessian

Metal foil paper

Surface covering defects

Figure 10.9 shows some common types of surface covering defects that can occur.

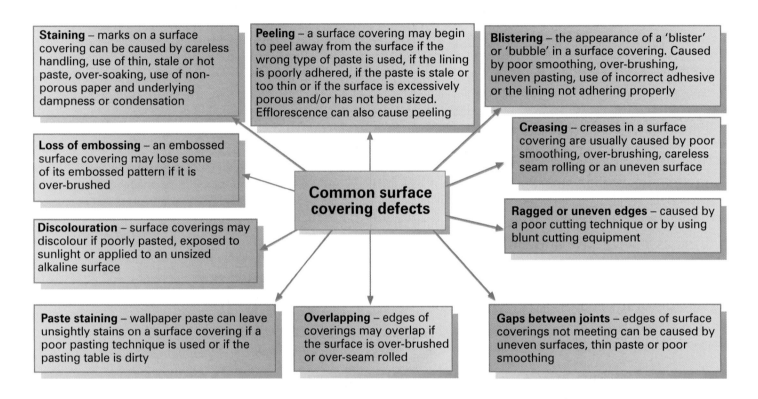

Staining – marks on a surface covering can be caused by careless handling, use of thin, stale or hot paste, over-soaking, use of non-porous paper and underlying dampness or condensation

Peeling – a surface covering may begin to peel away from the surface if the wrong type of paste is used, if the lining is poorly adhered, if the paste is stale or too thin or if the surface is excessively porous and/or has not been sized. Efflorescence can also cause peeling

Blistering – the appearance of a 'blister' or 'bubble' in a surface covering. Caused by poor smoothing, over-brushing, uneven pasting, use of incorrect adhesive or the lining not adhering properly

Loss of embossing – an embossed surface covering may lose some of its embossed pattern if it is over-brushed

Discolouration – surface coverings may discolour if poorly pasted, exposed to sunlight or applied to an unsized alkaline surface

Common surface covering defects

Creasing – creases in a surface covering are usually caused by poor smoothing, over-brushing, careless seam rolling or an uneven surface

Ragged or uneven edges – caused by a poor cutting technique or by using blunt cutting equipment

Paste staining – wallpaper paste can leave unsightly stains on a surface covering if a poor pasting technique is used or if the pasting table is dirty

Overlapping – edges of coverings may overlap if the surface is over-brushed or over-seam rolled

Gaps between joints – edges of surface coverings not meeting can be caused by uneven surfaces, thin paste or poor smoothing

Figure 10.9 Surface covering defects

FAQ

Nobody seems to have wallpaper in their house anymore – why do I have to learn how to hang it?

It is true that wallpaper isn't as popular as it once was, but as with many fashions and trends, the popularity of wallpaper will probably increase at some point during your career as a painter and decorator. When this happens, you will be glad you know how to hang it!

Why is wallpaper paste sometimes lumpy?

Because it hasn't been mixed up properly! Wallpaper paste should always be smooth. Make sure you read and follow the instructions on the packaging.

On the job: Mixing wallpaper paste

Phillip is at a client's house about to decorate a room in a new extension. The client has requested wallpaper and Phillip is getting his equipment ready to mix up some wallpaper paste. Phillip can't find his mixing stick and so he decides to mix up the paste using his hand.

Do you think Phillip has planned well for this job? What do you think of Phillip's idea to mix the paste by hand?

Knowledge check

1. Give two reasons why surface coverings should not be applied to greasy or dirty surfaces.

2. How should nail and screw heads be treated during surface preparation?

3. Why should starch paste not be used to size plaster surfaces before papering?

4. What can be applied to plasterboard prior to papering to protect it from damage when coverings are removed?

5. Briefly describe two methods of estimating the amount of paper that will be required for a job.

6. When might you use the following types of adhesive: border adhesive; Lincrusta glue; overlap adhesive?

7. Why is it important to check the batch numbers on rolls of wallpaper?

8. Name and describe two types of wallpaper folding technique. When would each be used?

9. What is 'centralising a wallpaper pattern'?

10. What is preparatory paper?

11. Name four types of specialist surface covering. In what circumstances might each be used?

12. Name four different types of common surface coating defect and explain how each may be caused.

Table 10.6 Basic types of wallpaper

Lining paper *A smooth preparatory paper available in a range of grades. Usually off-white, but brown and red lining papers are available as a base for coloured finish papers*	**Uses** As a base for finish papers of even porosity or as a base for painting. Masks minor surface defects and is especially suitable for well-prepared surfaces **Suitable wallpaper paste** Starch or cellulose **Preparation and hanging** Paste and allow paper to become supple before hanging. If used as a preparatory paper, it is usually hung horizontally to avoid the edges of the lining paper and finish paper falling in the same place **Other information** Available in 400, 600, 800 and 1000 grades in 200 mm and 555 mm wide single, double, triple or quad rolls
Non-woven lining paper *Made from cellulose and polyester fibre. Most common weight is 150 g*	**Uses** On surfaces that may move, such as tongue and grooved cladding or badly-cracked plaster **Suitable wallpaper paste** Starch or tub paste **Preparation and hanging** No need to soak. The wall can sometimes be pasted instead of the paper
Patterned pulp paper *A flat, standard wallpaper made from wood pulp, with a design printed on the surface. Many different qualities available ranging from simple machine-printed wallpaper to expensive hand-printed wallpaper*	**Uses** General living areas such as living rooms, bedrooms and staircases **Suitable wallpaper paste** Cellulose **Preparation and hanging** Check batch numbers and shade prior to hanging **Other information** Some patterned pulps have a coating of PVA varnish and are known as 'washables' because they can be sponged to remove stains

Anaglypta® textured paper *A brand name for an embossed paper made from wood pulp. A preparatory paper which requires painting*	**Uses** Ceilings and walls in domestic premises. Masks minor surface defects **Suitable wallpaper paste** Starch paste, cellulose (thick) **Preparation and hanging** Over-soaking, over-brushing joints and the use of seam rollers will flatten the embossed pattern. Always leave a hairline gap at the joints, which can later be flooded with paint to provide an invisible joint **Other information** Can be used as an alternative to blown vinyl (see below)
Vinyl paper *Made from a PVC (type of plastic) layer joined to a pulp backing paper. A very hard-wearing wallpaper*	**Uses** Domestic and commercial premises where there is heavy human traffic. Kitchens, bathrooms or areas where there is condensation **Suitable wallpaper paste** Cellulose can be used, but tub paste is a better choice. Overlap adhesive is required on overlaps. Ready-pasted paper is widely available **Preparation and hanging** Always read the manufacturer's instructions. Can be smoothed out with a smoothing brush or a caulking tool. Stanley knives and a straight edge can be used to speed up the trimming process **Other information** Can be sponged to remove marks and stains. Can be peeled off and is easy to strip
Blown vinyl paper *A textured layer of PVC-bonded paper. There are two basic types: a textured preparatory paper that can be used as an alternative to Anaglypta® and needs to be painted and a textured and coloured finish paper that can be used as an alternative to embossed, patterned pulp*	**Uses** Domestic and commercial premises. Not suitable in areas with heavy human traffic because the relief design can be easily damaged **Suitable wallpaper paste** Cellulose can be used, but tub paste is a better choice. Overlap adhesive is required on overlaps **Preparation and hanging** Apply with a smoothing brush. Avoid overlaps on internal/external angles by back trimming (double cutting)

Table 10.7 Specialist surface coverings

Cloth-backed vinyl *Made of PVC on a cotton scrim backing. The vinyl is either printed with a pattern or self-coloured and textured to look like fabric*	**Trimming** Knife and steel straight edge. Leave untrimmed **Pasting** Use an adhesive containing a fungicide as the vinyl is water resistant and the paste will not be able to dry out through the material. Paste the cloth either with brush, roller or spread with filling knife. Paste the wall **Hanging** Fold and hang to a plumb line and butt all joints. Use the rounded edge of a plastic squeegee to smooth the material and smooth out all air from behind. Excess paste will be squeezed out at the edges, which must be immediately rinsed off. Paste the wall just beyond the width of material. Offer up the material dry and smooth down with squeegee. Paste the next section of wall and place the next length slightly overlapping the previous length before smoothing down. Place straight edge in line with the centre of the overlap and cut through the two thicknesses using a trimming knife and a 'first time cut'. Lift up the edges and take out the trimmings, then 'liven' the edges with paste and smooth down to a butt joint. Special tools are available for cutting through the overlaps that do not require a straight edge. **Other information** Has a repeated pattern that the decorator may need to match. Available in 30 m x 1 m wide rolls and can be purchased by the metre.

Lincrusta-Walton	
Has a raised pattern or texture, which is created by rolling a putty-like substance onto a continuous reel of heavy cartridge paper. The putty is embossed onto the surface while the paper back remains flat. Textures commonly produced are hessian and wood in sheet and plank form. Requires painting after hanging	**Trimming** Knife and straight edge, undercut. **Pasting** Use Lincrusta glue. Paste on the paper back. **Hanging** Cut into lengths with a little in excess. Sponge several lengths of the paper backing with warm (not hot) water and leave to soak for 15–20 minutes, which will cause the paper to expand and will prevent blisters in the finished work. After soaking, sponge off any water and cut the expanded length to fit exactly. Apply Lincrusta glue to the backing. Hang with butt joints, smoothing down with a rubber roller using firm pressure and a vigorous action. When soaking and pasting, avoid sharp folds which may cause cracking of the surface. Lay lengths back-to-back when soaking which will help to retain moisture and achieve even expansion. External angles must be turned by cutting through the putty on the face (but not through the paper) exactly on the angle and bending the paper back around the angle. Any gaps on the angle can be filled with stiff linseed oil putty. Internal angles must be cut to fit exactly. **Painting** The surface is slightly oily and greasy and must be wiped off with white spirit before painting with oil-based paint (not emulsion). **Other information** Store rolls standing upright to avoid the weight cracking the face putty. Available in 1025 mm x 525 mm rolls; can also be supplied in panels and borders.

Woven glass fibre *White glass fibre woven into three textures: coarse, medium, fine. Generally used to reinforce cracked and imperfect surfaces and is then painted*	**Trimming** Knife and straight edge. Trim on wall **Pasting** Use PVA reinforced paste or PVA adhesive (straight). Paste the wall. **Hanging** Cut the lengths with 50 mm excess at top and bottom. Paste the wall evenly with a short pile paint roller, finishing a little short of the actual width of the glass fibre so that the edges of the first and second lengths overlap in a completely dry state. Hang the dry fabric and smooth down with a felt roller or plastic squeegee. Paste the second section of wall, again finishing a little short of the actual width. Cut through the overlap with a knife and straight edge, peeling away the two edges. Brush paste onto the 'missed' stripe of wall and press the two trimmed edges down as a perfect butt joint. If the wall is pasted to the full width of glass fibre then the edges will take in water and become too wet to obtain crisp, clean cutting, resulting in ragged joints. Trim the fabric to parallel widths on the pasteboard. Paste the wall to the entire width of the fabric. Hang dry, trimmed fabric, smoothing down with a felt roller. Paste the next section of wall surface and hang the next length of dry, trimmed fabric with a butt joint. Continue with the next length using the same method. **Other information** Available in 50 m x 1 m rolls and can be purchased by the metre

Paper-backed felt	**Trimming** Knife and straight edge. The main problem is making a first cut. If a blunt knife or not enough pressure is used, a second cut can make the edges very ragged. A clean cut first time gives perfect butt joints.
Made from a thick blanket of dyed short wool fibres	**Pasting** Use stiff tub paste or PVA reinforced adhesive. Paste the paper back.
	Hanging Very little soaking is required after pasting and folding the material. Hang to a plumb line with butt joints, smoothing down with a felt roller. Reverse alternate lengths to minimise the effect of any edge-to-edge shading. Angles can be turned in the normal way. If the fabric and paper are not too wet, cutting to top and bottom and around obstacles can be done with a template and knife. If paper-backed felt is too wet, either allow to dry off and then cut with a template and knife, or mark with template and chalk and then cut with scissors.
	Other information Avoid getting paste on the cloth, which can damage it! Available in 50 m x 0.91 m rolls and can be purchased by the metre.
Paper-backed hessian	**Trimming** Knife and straight edge. The key to hanging hessian is clean first-time cutting when trimming the material. If a blunt knife or insufficient pressure is used and a second cut has to be taken, then the edges can become frayed. Two slightly frayed edges look very unsightly when butt jointed. Clean, first-time cutting hides the joint perfectly.
Made of jute which can be dyed and then woven, or woven into cloth and then dyed. Laminated onto a paper back	**Pasting** Use stiff tub paste or PVA reinforced paste. Paste the paper back.
	Hanging Very little soaking is necessary after pasting and folding the material. Hang to a plumb line while smoothing down with a felt roller. Reverse alternate lengths to minimise the effect of any edge-to-edge shading.

	Angles can be turned in the normal way. If the fabric and paper are not too wet, cutting to top and bottom and around obstacles can be done with a template and knife. If too wet, either allow to dry off before cutting, or mark with template and chalk and cut with scissors. **Other information** Avoid getting paste on the cloth, which can damage it! Available in 50 m x 0.91 m rolls and can be purchased by the metre
Paper-backed laminated foils *A surface covering made from several thin layers, namely: paper (as the backing), a metal or mirror-like finish (foil) and a laminated top layer*	**Trimming** Knife and straight edge. Undercut slightly. **Pasting** Some foils are straightforward laminates of tarnished metal leaves, or figured and engraved continuous sheets applied onto a paper backing. These present no problem when pasted and hung in the normal way except for a curling of the edges similar to cork veneer papers. See type 1 foils below. Other foils with burnished mirror-like backgrounds present many problems. The mirror-like background magnifies every tiny defect behind the foil so preparation must be perfect. If the foil backing is pasted, even the paste brush marks can damage the finish. Paste must be applied evenly to the wall with a short pile paint roller and the stipple effect allowed to flow out before offering up the dry material. See type 2 foils below *Type 1 foils*: Paste the material *Type 2 foils*: Paste the wall once or twice with PVA adhesive (must contain a fungicide) Some highly reflective foils are also laminated to include a plastic membrane – these curl badly if pasted. Even when dry they are very stiff and the curl from the roll will not lie flat. Use a very sticky adhesive to hold this type of foil. This can be achieved by pasting the wall twice.

	Hanging
	Type 1 foils: Fold down without creasing, then hang to a plumb line and butt all joints. Smooth down with felt or rubber roller. Cut to top and bottom and around obstacles in the normal way with scissors
	Type 2 foils: Paste the wall once or twice as necessary, allow stipple texture to flow out and hang the dry foil to a plumb line, then butt all joints. Smooth down with felt or rubber roller. Cut to top and bottom and around obstacles with plastic template and knife. Remove any paste immediately from the surface after fixing with a soft sponge, and polish dry with a very soft cloth.
	Other information Available in 7.31 m x 0.91 m rolls
Hand-printed papers *Many of today's hand prints are produced by silkscreen printing, and have large patterns*	**Trimming** Knife and steel straight edge. Undercut
	Pasting Use stiff tub paste and PVA reinforced pastes. Paste the paper.
	Hanging Select a good top and centre the pattern on important features. Take care not to crease the folds after pasting. Most modern papers are printed with waterfast inks and will not smear, but there are still some delicate papers that will spoil if paste comes into contact with the face. Always smooth the paper with a felt roller to prevent polishing and breaking the edges. Avoid the use of a seam roller which will only tend to polish the joints. Cut at top and bottom and around obstacles in the normal way with scissors.
	Other information Available in 10.05 m x 0.525 m rolls

abrading (abrasion)	to wear away by rubbing
adhere	stick
adhesive	glue
alkaline	having a pH greater than 7 (an acid has a pH of less than 7)
architrave	a decorative moulding, usually made from timber, that is fitted around door and window frames to hide the gap between the frame and the wall
atomised	when a liquid is broken up into tiny droplets like a mist
barrier cream	a cream used to protect the skin from damage or infection
bitumen	a heavy, semi-solid, brown-black substance also known as asphalt or tar
burnishing	polishing
carded scaffolder	someone who holds a recognised certificate showing competence in scaffold erection
combustion	burning or catching on fire
conservation	preservation of the environment and wildlife
contamination	when harmful chemicals or substances pollute something (e.g. water)
corroded	destroyed or damaged by a chemical reaction
corrosive	a substance that can damage things it comes into contact with (e.g. material, skin)
coving	a decorative moulding that is fitted at the top of a wall where it meets the ceiling
crawling board	a board or platform placed on roof joists which spread the weight of the worker allowing roof work to be carried out safely
damp proof course	a substance that is used to prevent damp from penetrating a building
decant	to pour liquid from one container to another

decorator's crutch	a rolled-up length of wallpaper or a piece of wood used to support a concertina fold
dermatitis	a skin condition whereby the affected area is red, itchy and sore
driers	a liquid chemical that promotes drying
drop match	a wallpaper pattern that is not repeated horizontally across the paper
durable	long-lasting
egress	an exit or way out
embossed	(wallpaper) decorated with designs that stand out from the surface
employer	the person or company you work for
enforced	making sure a law is obeyed
equal stretch	(of wallpaper lengths) supple and pliable to the same degree
filling	the bristles of a paint brush
flush	when one surface is level and even with another surface
hazard	a danger or risk
Health and Safety Executive (HSE)	the government organisation that enforces health and safety law in the UK
induction	a formal introduction you will receive when you start any new job, where you will be shown around, shown where the toilets and canteen etc. are, and told what to do if there is a fire
inverted	tipped and turned upside down
jute	a rough fibre made from a tropical plant used in paper-backed Hessian wallpaper
key	roughness on a surface provided to aid adhesion
Lincrusta-Walton	a wall-hanging with a relief pattern used to imitate wood panelling
lint	tiny, fuzzy fibres of material
LPG	liquefied petroleum gas
mildew	a fungus that grows in damp conditions

millscale	a scale that forms on steel
mordant	a substance that provides
solution	a key
muster points	fire assembly points
noxious	harmful or poisonous
permeable	allowing liquids and gases to pass through
plant	industrial machinery
plaster skim	a thin layer of plaster that is put on to walls to give a smooth and even finish
plumb bob	a weight attached to string or twine used to produce a vertical line
porosity	the ability of a surface to allow water through
pot life	the amount of time paint remains at a workable consistency
proactive	taking action *before* something happens (e.g. an accident)
proportionately	in proportion to the size of something else
prosecute	to accuse someone of committing a crime, which usually results in being taken to court and, if found guilty, being punished
PVC	polyvinyl chloride (a type of plastic)
rabbit skin size	a substance made from animal tissues, which is applied before a later of varnish on a gilded surface
reactive	taking action *after* something happens
relief material	a material that has a pattern that stands out from the background
rendering	stone or brickwork coated with plaster
resin	a natural or man-made material used as a binder in paint
restoration	returning a building to its original condition
rust	a red or yellowish-brown coating of iron oxide

sanitise	to make something clean and free of germs
saponification	a chemical reaction that makes soap and so foams up as a result
scumble	a semi-transparent stain or glaze applied over a hard, dry ground coat
scuttle	a special container for paint used when painting from a ladder with a roller
size	seal
skinning	the formation of a skin on paint which occurs when the top layer dries out
skirting	a decorative moulding that is fitted at the bottom of a wall to hide the gap between the wall and the floor
spot prime	the application of primer (base coat) to small areas
stiles	the side pieces of a stepladder into which the steps are set
straight match	a wallpaper design that is repeated horizontally across the paper
symptom	a sign of illness or disease (e.g. difficulty breathing, a sore hand or a lump under the skin)
tie-rods	metal rods underneath the rungs of a ladder that give extra support to the rungs
toxic	poisonous
truss	prefabricated component of a roof which spreads the load of the roof over the outer walls and forms its shape
vibration white finger	a condition that can be caused by using vibrating machinery (usually for very long periods of time). The blood supply to the fingers is reduced which causes pain, tingling and sometimes spasms (shaking)